TREASURES OF DURHAM UNIVERSITY LIBRARY

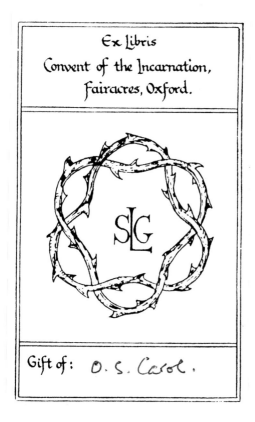

Non minima pars eruditionis est bonos nosse libros
Not the least part of erudition is to be acquainted with good books

Manuale ſcholarium

qui ſtudentium vniuerſitates aggredi. ac poſtea proficere in eiſdem intendunt

Treasures of Durham University Library

Edited by Richard Gameson

Durham University

III Third Millennium Publishing, London

IPPONNOSTICON LAURENTII DUNELMEN
SIS MONACHI. DE VETERI ET NOVO
TESTAMENTO INCIPIT.

deus.

PRINCIPIU[M] reru[m] sine te[m]pore te[m]pora formans.
Et formata regens. Regnat ubiq[ue] deus.
Qui pat[er] et p[ro]les seu flaminis una potestas.
Unum s[ed] trinum: nomina trina notant.
Alter enim pater e[st]. qui[n] filius alter eorum.
Sp[iritu]s estq[ue] tamen. Quisq[ue] q[uo]d alter idem.
Respice p[er]sonas. trinumq[ue] fatere. s[ed] unum.
Par decus. et deitas indicat una deum.
Si numerare velis: iterare uocabula trina.
Hic potes. Ipse tamen tres numerare nequis.
Cunq[ue] sit una salus. honor un[us] et una voluntas.
His tribus: hii tres sunt. unus ubiq[ue] deus.

De Coniunctione Elementorum.

Qui uariis elementa locis aptauit ut aer.
Igne sit inferior. terraq[ue] substet aquis.
Neue repugnet eis. in eis q[uo]d dissonat: aptis
Et sibi cognatis nexibus illa ligat.

De Ornamentis Elementorum.

Alter exposito rerum fundamine: multos
Addidit ornatus actibus ipse suis.
Stellaru[m] rutilo fulgore uolubile celum.
Et micat et uariis motibus astra meant.
Terra ferax nemorum. noua floribus herbida p[ra]ta.
Fructibus eximium. p[ro]misit opima situm.
Grataq[ue] temp[er]ies: dat aeris. equor: amenum
Dum fluit ac refluit: dat sine fine iocum.

Unde sint singulorum elementorum animantia creata.
Et simul herba forent animalibus unda carq[ue]:
Paruit. et pisces protulit. hec et aues.
Ipsa fouet pisces. auis exit in aera. cedit
Terra feris. Celum: Cetibus angelicis.
Terra q[uo]d edit: habet. p[ri]ma s[ed] origine rerum
Angel[u]s ex nichilo conditus: alta tenet

De Essentia Angelorum.

[title page]
Manuale scholarium. *Cologne: Heinrich Quentell, c. 1495 (SR.2.A.19)*

[previous page]
In this mid-twelfth-century manuscript of the works of Laurence, prior of Durham 1149-54, the text of his Hypognosticon *is prefaced by a depiction of a monk writing, doubtless meant to represent the author himself. Though stylised, the image provides valuable insight into the practicalities of scribal work in the twelfth century. Laurence's cunningly-wrought chair is in fact a type of writing stool that is well known from later depictions and which, resembling a baby's 'high-chair', was equipped with an adjustable desk supported by a pair of arms that slotted into either side of the frame. The open book on the desk-surface is artistic licence (a scribe would generally have worked on individual sheets of parchment), but the other tools – an awl (stuck into the desk), a knife (in the scribe's left hand) and a trimmed quill pen (in his right one) – are accurate. The awl was used to mark the sheets with rows of prickings to guide the horizontal ruled lines that supported the writing (clearly visible in catalogue nos. 3 and 4). The knife was used for corrections (literally scraping off the offending letters and words: see nos. 3 and 7) and as a means of supporting the scribe's writing hand. For good scribes, like the depicted Laurence, would write with their hands held above the surface of the page in order to avoid oil deposited from their skin interfering with the adhesion of the ink. See further no. 4.*
Cosin MS V. iii. 1, fols. 22v-3r

TREASURES OF DURHAM UNIVERSITY LIBRARY

First published in 2007 by
Third Millennium Publishing Limited,
a subsidiary of Third Millennium Information Limited.

2–5 Benjamin Street
London
United Kingdom
EC1M 5QL
www.tmiltd.com

ISBN 978 1 903942 74 1

Edited by Richard Gameson
Designed by Susan Pugsley
Production by Bonnie Murray

Reprographics by Asia Graphic Printing Ltd
Printed & bound in Italy by Printer Trento

Right: Entrance to Bamburgh Library

BAMBURGH LIBRARY

Contents

Foreword

Living as we do in an age in which books are cheap and abundantly available everywhere – even now in supermarkets – it is easy to forget what wondrous and valued instruments they once were.

For much of their history books were things of beauty in their own right, and at least as valuable to their owners as furniture and paintings – often very much more so. Medieval manuscripts were not only hugely labour-intensive, but were great consumers of costly materials, and much the same could be said of printed books for at least their first two hundred years. Yet unlike paintings and other works of art, books were also repositories of knowledge and learning and collective thought, which gave them an additional, unquantifiable value. Books not only provided aesthetic satisfaction, but could also be kept for diversion, instruction, devotion, record keeping.

So books have always been prized, and one of the greatest collections in England, I am proud to tell you, is to be found at Durham. Surprisingly few people, including many within the university itself, are aware of just how extensive and diverse the University Library's holdings are. Yet Durham quietly holds, and lovingly maintains, one of the largest collections of medieval manuscripts in Britain, as well as no fewer than seventy thousand books printed before 1850. Among the former is a volume of Chaucer's *Troilus* and *Criseyde* from the mid-fifteenth century, among the latter a first edition of Thomas More's *Utopia*, a copy of Bacon's *Essays* (with the most exquisite embroidered cover) and several works from the London workshop of Wynkyn de Worde, surely the most pleasingly named printer in history.

And on top of all that, Durham also holds – unexpectedly but endearingly – the largest Sudanese archive in the world outside Sudan.

This is clearly a collection worth knowing. So it is a very real joy to welcome here such a handsome and readable survey – all the more so as its publication happily coincides with the University's 175th anniversary. What better way to mark the venerability of the university than by celebrating the even greater venerability of its books?

Bill Bryson

Werner Rolevinck, Fasciculus temporum omnes antiquorum cronicas complectans. *Strasbourg: Johann Prüss, not before 1490 (SR.2.A.13).*

PREFACE

Universities are remarkable places. They bring together people with a huge range of diverse and wonderful interests and provide an opportunity for them to work together to evaluate existing knowledge, to innovate, and to disseminate the findings. Nowhere else would you find such a range of special interests and expertise coupled with a spirit of curiosity, imagination and creativity.

Add to this the incalculable resource of a major library, where the wisdom of many others over the centuries is collected, and one has a unique combination. Supplement this with the electronic resources of the digital age and scholars world-wide are connected to each other – an international alliance of knowledge.

Universities are about ideas. Now, ideas should not sit in boxes – the province of the few scholars who happen to know about the contents of the box – they need to be shared, discussed and debated with people from a wide variety of disciplines. Moreover, this debate extends far beyond the walls of the 'Ivory Towers', beyond individual scholars and disciplines, to engage the public in the wider world. The present volume embodies these principles: the wide range of specialists who have contributed reflects the wealth of expertise; while the items treated – fifty selected from amongst thousands – illustrate just how much interesting material is available, how fascinating are the topics they raise, and how multidisciplinary they are.

Books provide the common focus. These are the vehicles through which the ideas of previous generations can be explored, and from which new ideas can be generated. They are a precious resource to be cared for, cherished, and shared. Durham University Library, with its numerous historic collections – containing material that ranges in date from Antiquity to the present, that reflects many different parts of the globe, and that has been deposited by ecclesiastics and scientists, scholars and politicians, institutions and private individuals, united by their concern for the preservation and transmission of knowledge and culture – is a flagship in this respect, typifying the centrality and vibrancy of learning for society.

Alongside exotic material from the Sudan, from Europe and from elsewhere, the present selection of treasures includes several items of exceptional interest from Durham and its environs, alluding to the firm relationship between the University and its region. Reaching out to the community in the North East of England and beyond is a clear part of our remit. In the year of our 175th anniversary this volume will make accessible the Treasures of our Library and encourage others to use it and celebrate its richness.

Kenneth C. Calman

Woodcut illustration tipped into [Thomas More, Contra*]* insanas Lutheri calumnias *(**no. 27**).*

Ipse dixit et fa
sũt ipse mãdauit
Ps 32
creata sũt
non inferiora secutus

Acknowledgments

Production of this volume was made possible by a generous gift from Peter Holland, with further support from the Western Manuscripts / History of the Book project funding, sponsors of which include the Foyle Foundation.

The present enterprise has, throughout, been a work of collaboration between the editor and the Head of Heritage Collections, Sheila Hingley, supported by the staff of Archives and Special Collections. The photography of the principal items was the work of Kate Weightman, additional images being supplied by Michelle Brown, Sheila Hingley and Richard Gameson. The editor also received invaluable assistance at key junctures from Fiona, Christine and Brian Gameson.

General enquiries about the Special Collections and access thereto should be addressed to: Palace Green Library, Palace Green, Durham DH1 3RN; pg.library@durham.ac.uk . Enquiries about teaching and research on Western Manuscripts and the History of the Book may be directed to: richard.gameson@durham.ac.uk.

Left: Pictorial frontispiece to the main text of Hartmann Schedel, Liber chronicorum *(**no. 21**): God the Creator with the legend, 'He spoke and they were made; he commanded and they were created' (Psalm 32.9).*

Professor Airy
DURHAM ZEPHYRS
De gustibus non est disputandum
"Blow wind & crack your cheeks!
" INCUTE VIM VENTIS × × OBRUE PUPP(I)ES." ÆN: I. 69.
~ Designed Etched & Published by Edward Bradley Feby 20th 1849 ~

Contributors

David Ashurst, Dept. of English Studies
Jenny Britnell, Dept. of French
Richard Britnell, Dept. of History
David Brown, Dept. of Theology and Religion
Bill Bryson, Chancellor
Kenneth C. Calman, Vice-Chancellor 1998–2007
Neil Cartlidge, Dept. of English Studies
Robert H. F. Carver, Dept. of English Studies
Martin Daly, Waterville, Maine
Jeremy Dibble, Dept. of Music
A. I. Doyle, Honorary Reader in Bibliography
M. D. Eddy, Dept. of Philosophy
Richard Gameson, Dept. of History
Giles Gasper, Dept. of History
Ingo Gildenhard, Dept. of Classics and Ancient History
J. T. D. Hall, University Librarian
Carol Harrison, Dept. of Theology and Religion
P. D. A. Harvey, Dept. of History
Alan Heesom, Dept. of History
Richard Higgins, Archives and Special Collections
Sheila Hingley, Archives and Special Collections
David Knight, Dept. of Philosophy
Andrew Louth, Dept. of Theology and Religion
Peter Maber, Trinity College, Cambridge
Richard Maber, Dept. of French
John McKinnell, Dept. of English Studies
Natalie Mears, Dept. of History
Ann Moss, Dept. of French
L. V. Pitcher, Dept. of Classics and Ancient History
Christopher Prior, Dept. of History
Stephen Regan, Dept. of English Studies
J. T. Rhodes, former librarian of Ushaw College, Durham
David Rollason, Dept. of History
Michael Sadgrove, Dean of Durham Cathedral
Corinne Saunders, Dept. of English Studies
Geoffrey Scarre, Dept. of Philosophy
Michael Stansfield, Archives and Special Collections
Jane Taylor, Dept. of French
David Thomas, Dept. of Classics and Ancient History
J. R. Watson, Dept. of English Studies
Arnold Wolfendale, Dept. of Physics

*'Durham Zephyrs': sketch of Palace Green by Edward Bradley, 1849 (**no. 41**).*

INTRODUCTION

Durham, site of the third oldest university in England (after Oxford and Cambridge), has been a seat of learning for much longer than it has been a university city. The ecclesiastical foundation which developed on the peninsula, following the migration of a group of monks from Lindisfarne, led to Durham becoming both a cultural centre and a political stronghold for the Prince Bishops. The monk Symeon who wrote a history of the church of Durham (see no. 3) was one of many associated with the Benedictine priory in Durham whose life embraced learning and scholarship. If the discussions about founding a university in the city that arose in the Commonwealth period came to nothing, the essential part of such an institution – a library – was established shortly afterwards by John Cosin. A book-collector throughout his life, Cosin went into exile to Paris in 1644, acting as chaplain to the court of Queen Henrietta Maria; having left his library behind in Cambridge, he began to assemble a new collection, which, when he returned to England at the Restoration, he brought with him. As Bishop of Durham (1660–72), Cosin conceived the idea of building for local clergy and scholars an endowed public library, which was founded in 1669.

Cosin's library, which is still housed in its original building, has been at the heart of the University since its foundation in 1832. Essentially the bishop's own books, including manuscripts by himself, his associates and contemporaries, the collection also includes gifts from other benefactors, notably medieval manuscripts from George Davenport, and the antiquarian manuscripts of the

LIII
LIV

Above: Vault in Exchequer Building.
Left: John Cosin (full length portrait in Cosin's Library).

Mickleton and Spearman families given in 1817 by Shute Barrington, bishop of Durham. The medieval manuscript books include theological, liturgical, legal, historical, medical, scientific and culinary texts (see nos. 2–6, 8–11, 13–15). Amongst more than 5,000 printed items, the strongest areas are theology, liturgy and canon law, with a good representation of such other subjects as literature, travel and science. There is a large group of French publications, many extremely rare, collected during Cosin's exile in Paris (see no. 31). A notable treasure is the 1619 *Book of Common Prayer*, annotated with Cosin's proposals for the 1662 revision (no. 33). Vested in the University as trustee in 1937, this library – building and contents – was awarded 'designated status' in 2005.

Durham University was founded in 1832 through the efforts of William Van Mildert, bishop of Durham, and Charles Thorp, rector of Ryton and one of the prebendaries of Durham Cathedral, who well understood the political expediency of a wealthy church taking the lead in establishing a northern university. In many ways the development of the University Library parallels that of the University itself, the growth of the collections mirroring its expansion. The foundation collection, presented by Van Mildert on 1 January 1833, was lodged in Cosin's library, in a gallery erected at the bishop's expense. Clearly Van Mildert wanted the fledgling university to flourish, and he may have encouraged a number of the early donations to its library from members of the Durham chapter and other local churchmen.

The most significant donation to date arrived in Durham in 1855. Martin Joseph Routh (1755–1854), patristics scholar and president of Magdalen College, Oxford, had made a deed of gift in March 1852, 'being desirous that the library I have collected may serve the purpose of promoting the glory of God through advancement of good learning, and feeling a deep interest in the recently established University of Durham, as likely to further the same important purpose'. His collection of almost 22,000 items was shelved on the top floor of the fifteenth-century Exchequer building, where it remains today, presided over by a portrait and bust of the donor. Routh had inherited books from his father and was an assiduous collector throughout a very long life. A working library

Above: Cosin's Library in 1842: examinations (drawn by R. W. Buss; engraved by G. H. Adcock).
Left: Detail of bookcase in Cosin's Library, with portraits of Counter-Reformation authors, indicating content of case.

to support his scholarship and writing, its particular strengths are in patristics and scripture (no. 16), church history (no. 19), religious controversy (nos. 27–8), and English political controversy of the seventeenth and eighteenth centuries; but Routh was also a keen collector of pamphlet literature on all periods and aspects of English history, including such subjects as Catholic emancipation, the Oxford movement, and university reform.

In the same decade came two further great gifts – from Edward Maltby (1770–1859), bishop of Durham 1836–56, and Thomas Masterman Winterbottom (1766–1859), physician, of South Shields. In the former, Classical literature, philology, and theology are prominent, with some science and English literature, including

Above: Bishop Cosin's Library and Exchequer Building from Palace Green.
Left: Cosin's arms, above the doorway to his library. The accompanying motto (not shown in full) is quoted on p. 1.

Sir Thomas Browne's *Hydriotaphia* (1658) with an inscription and corrections by the author (no. 32). There are also books that might not be expected in a library of this kind, such as Captain John Smith's *General history of Virginia* (1624). In the latter, travel literature (especially on Africa and Asia) and natural science are particular strengths. The Maltby and Winterbottom collections occupied the Chancery and Cursitor's rooms in the Exchequer building, on the floor below Routh's library.

A landmark in the twentieth century was the deposit of the Sharp library from Bamburgh Castle, Northumberland, now referred to as the Bamburgh Library. Based on the acquisitions of three generations of the Sharp family, the bulk of the books passed in the late eighteenth century to the Trustees of Lord Crewe's Charity, who maintained the collection as a public library at Bamburgh Castle until 1958, when it was transferred to Durham University Library and placed in the Chancery Room of the Exchequer Building. Comprising some 8,500 miscellaneous titles, the collection has been likened to a college library of the eighteenth century, with good holdings of theology and classics along with English literature, as well as an emphasis on mathematics and

Left: Device of Wynkyn de Worde (Bamburgh Select 99; see ***no. 22****).*
Below: Bamburgh Library.

natural science. This final class includes first editions of Newton, Boyle, Ray and other members of the Royal Society, along with later works such as Selby's *Birds* (no. 39). The earliest items include medieval manuscripts (nos. 7 and 12), a rare Caxton (no. 18), and choice examples of the printing of Wynkyn de Worde (no. 22).

Throughout the history of the University Library, shortage of space has been a continual problem. As the holdings grew, the facility gradually expanded into adjacent buildings on the west side of Palace Green, adapting and linking existing structures. Then, during the second half of the twentieth-century there were considerable expansions to the system and space as a whole. In 1950, following the foundation of Oriental Studies in Durham, the oriental section of the Library was established, first in Old Elvet,

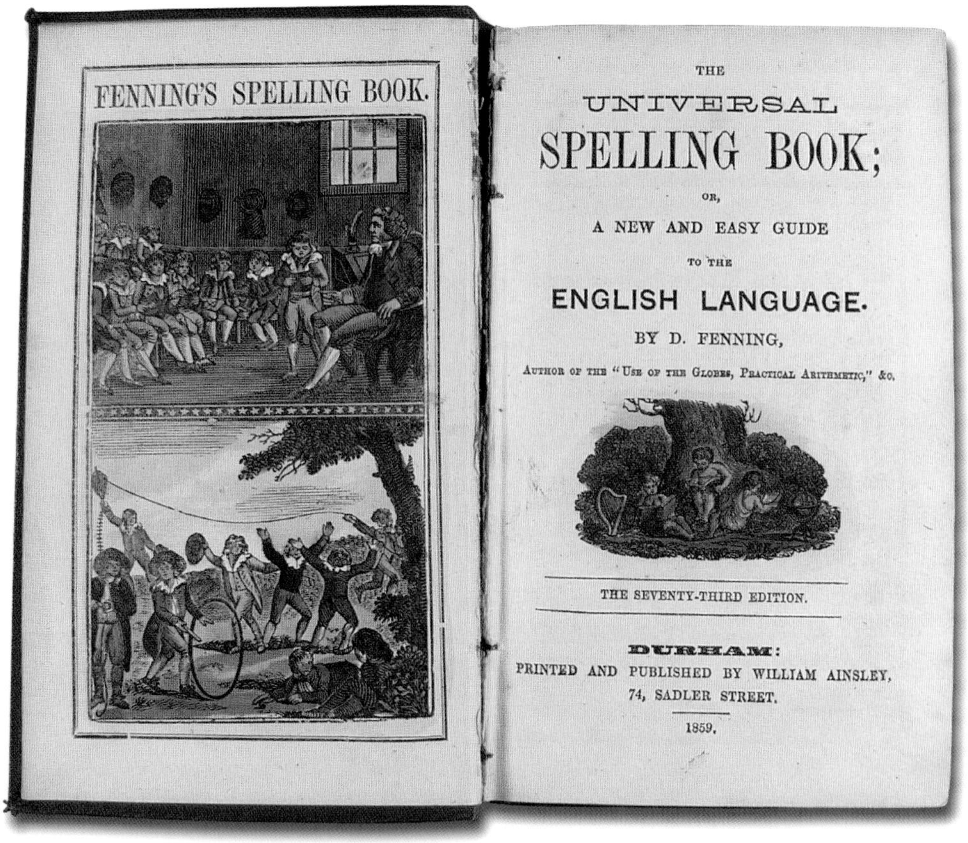

Daniel Fenning, The Universal Spelling Book; or a new and easy guide to the English language, 73rd ed. *(Durham, 1859): printed and published by Willam Ainsley (d. 1875), one of Durham's most prominent Victorian booksellers. XL 428 FEN.*

then South End House before the move to Elvet Hill House, where it remained until its amalgamation into the main library in 1987. A new science library, designed by Sir William Whitfield, opened in 1965; while a major extension to the Palace Green library designed by George Pace (who had previously worked on a restoration of Bishop Cosin's building) was occupied in 1966.

The inexorable growth of both University and Library led to further major changes less than twenty years later. As the constrained site at Palace Green could offer no prospect of further expansion, the Science library was extended and the locus of operations shifted from Palace Green to Stockton Road. The new central library opened in 1983, leaving at Palace Green the holdings for law and music, together with the special collections. Concommittently, the Department of Palaeography and Diplomatic, which had shared the Stockton Road building since its opening, moved to 5 The College, within the Cathedral precincts. The Department had been established in the immediate aftermath of the Second World War to care for the Cathedral muniments (then in the Prior's Kitchen) but, as its creation predated the local county record offices, it also provided a home to important regional archives, including those from the Baker Baker, Backhouse and Shafto families, and the estate papers of the Howards of Naworth. The Cathedral muniments were moved to 5 The College in 1992, shortly after the Department of Palaeography merged with the Library's special collections. The main library was extended in 1996, as part of a national building programme for university libraries, and proposals for further much-needed expansion are currently being developed.

Of the riches of the collections today only a summary overview, focusing on certain key areas, may be given here. One of the largest of the extensive archival holdings is the Durham Diocesan Archive, whose items extend in date from 1494 up to the present. These records of diocesan administration are supplemented by many associated collections, such as the Auckland Castle Episcopal Records, Church Commission deposits relating to the Bishopric Estates, the Durham Halmote Court Records about copyhold land and tenants on the estates of the bishopric, the Durham Probate Records, and numerous architectural drawings relating to church property. If collectively these form a major resource for ecclesiastical and Anglican history at local and national level, there is also much to support local history more generally, along with genealogy, legal studies, economic, social, educational and demographic history, dialect and place-name studies, and archaeological, architectural and geographical research.

Another major archival group is the Sudan Archive, a collection of the papers of former officials, soldiers, missionaries, business men and individuals who served or lived in the Sudan during the Anglo-Egyptian Condominium period (1898–1955) (see nos. 44, 46–7, 50). The archive, awarded 'designated status' in 2005, was begun in 1957 by Richard Hill, former official of the Sudan Government Railways, and a lecturer in the School of Oriental Studies at Durham. Knowing of numerous collections of private papers for which there was no suitable repository, Hill appealed to former officials of the Sudan Political Service and others to donate their material to Durham. The records range from official reports, memoranda and tribal histories to trek notes, personal letters, diaries and memoirs, along with extensive photographic holdings, cinefilms, maps, ephemera and artefacts. All levels of colonial society are represented, as are the technical and medical services, the army and the church. The largest of the more than 300 individual deposits within this archive is that of General Sir Reginald Wingate, successor to Kitchener as Governor-General of the Sudan. Supplemented by a comprehensive holding of printed materials, the archive continues to receive new material on a regular basis.

The Grey Papers, from the Earls Grey of Howick (including material from wives, daughters, younger sons and other relatives), constitute one of England's great political archives (see no. 40). Notable amongst this collection are the papers of Charles, 1st Earl

Part of the Routh collection on the top floor of the Exchequer building.

Right: Basil Bunting, Briggflatts *(London, c. 1966); copy 'K' of twenty-six special signed, lettered, leather-bound copies of the first edition. The script and decoration of this title-page are based upon the Lindisfarne Gospels of c. 700, the apogee of Northumbrian book art.*

Grey (1729–1807), which deal largely with military matters, especially the 1793–4 expedition to the West Indies; those of Charles, 2nd Earl Grey (1764–1845), reflecting his interest in parliamentary reform, Catholic emancipation and foreign affairs; and those of Henry George, 3rd Earl Grey (1802–94), significant for colonial history. Mention should also be made of the papers of Malcolm MacDonald (1901–81), cabinet minister, colonial governor and diplomat, also Chancellor of Durham University, which span his life; and those of Sir Donald Hawley, which cover his diplomatic career in Africa, the Middle East and the Far East.

Literary interests are well represented. The collection of literary manuscripts and correspondence formed by Claude Colleer Abbott (1889–1971), professor of English at the University 1932–54, being closely related to Abbott's research interests, focuses on George Darley, the Rossetti family and the Pre-Raphaelites, and the poet Edward Thomas (1878–1917) (see no. 43). In 1974 the manuscripts, papers, correspondence, photographs and library of William Plomer (1903–73), novelist, poet and librettist for Benjamin Britten, were presented by his literary executor, Sir Rupert Hart-Davis. Amidst extensive correspondence with prominent figures in the English literary world, this also includes one of the three surviving volumes of the diary of Francis Kilvert (no. 42). Such earlier gifts were considerably strengthened in 1987 by the establishment of the Basil Bunting Poetry Archive – a mixture of manuscripts, papers, printed material, recordings, videos and photographs, based on the collection of Bunting's bibliographer, Roger Guedalla – which continues to grow and is the most extensive in the country. The Basil Bunting Poetry Centre works alongside the archive, fostering academic projects associated with it and hosting visiting scholars and students.

A number of interesting collections of printed books have been acquired in recent years. In 1980 the Library received that of Dr C. E. Kellett (1908–78), a Newcastle historian of medicine from a north-eastern family. This illustrates the development of medical teaching and practice during the Renaissance, especially in France: the writings of the sixteenth-century French physician Jean Fernel and his circle, the classical and medieval sources on which they drew, and the later writers they influenced are well represented. In 1992 the remnants of the library of Lord William Howard (1563–1640), previously housed in his book-tower at Naworth Castle, Cumberland, were acquired at auction. Reflecting the owner's historical interests and Catholic faith, this includes an important group of historical and geographical works, a large number of religious texts and five commonplace books compiled by Henry Howard, Earl of Northampton (1540–1614). The Wilson Collection, bequeathed by Dudley Wilson (1923–95), professor of French at Durham, likewise reflects its collector's interests – in this case, literature and thought in the Renaissance and seventeenth century (particularly in France), along with typography and book illustration. One of the most recent acquisitions is the Whitehead Collection on

Red goatskin, gold-tooled binding by the so-called 'Geometrical Compartment Binder'; Het Boek der gemeene gebeden en bedieninge der Sacramenten *(London, 1704) – the Book of Common Prayer in Dutch (Bamburgh Select L.7.62).*

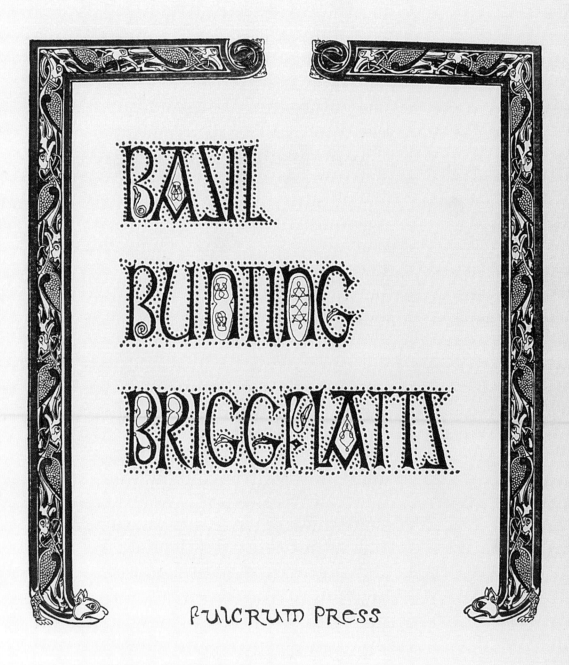

BASIL BUNTING

BRIGGFLATTS

FULCRUM PRESS

Left: Aerial view of Palace Green with Library (left foreground) and Castle.

deer, which supports the research in this area carried out in the School of Biological and Biomedical Sciences. Extensive in its coverage of deer (both in Britain and worldwide, particularly North America), it ranges much further to include the study of hunting, its broader implications, and its influence on weaponry and art.

Many other collections deserve mention – the manuscripts and books associated with the local polymath Thomas Wright (no. 37), other scientific holdings including the library of the Durham Observatory, material from the library of the mathematician and Chairman of the Durham University Council, Sir Edward Collingwood (1900–70), and books on the history of science given by Professor David Knight; the Pratt-Green hymnody collection (see no. 48), the Sunderland Friends library, the archive of the Cremation Society of Great Britain – but space prevents this. Yet paradoxically, such enforced omissions advertise the wealth of the holdings as a whole. Durham University is fortunate to have special collections of a breadth and depth that stand good comparison with other major university libraries, and are certainly the most important in the north east. The current volume, which picks highlights from a number of them, gives a sense of its riches: it is hoped that these 'snapshots' will stimulate further enquiry into Durham University Library's resources.

J. T. D. Hall

Interior of the reading room in the extension to the Palace Green Library by George Pace (completed 1966).

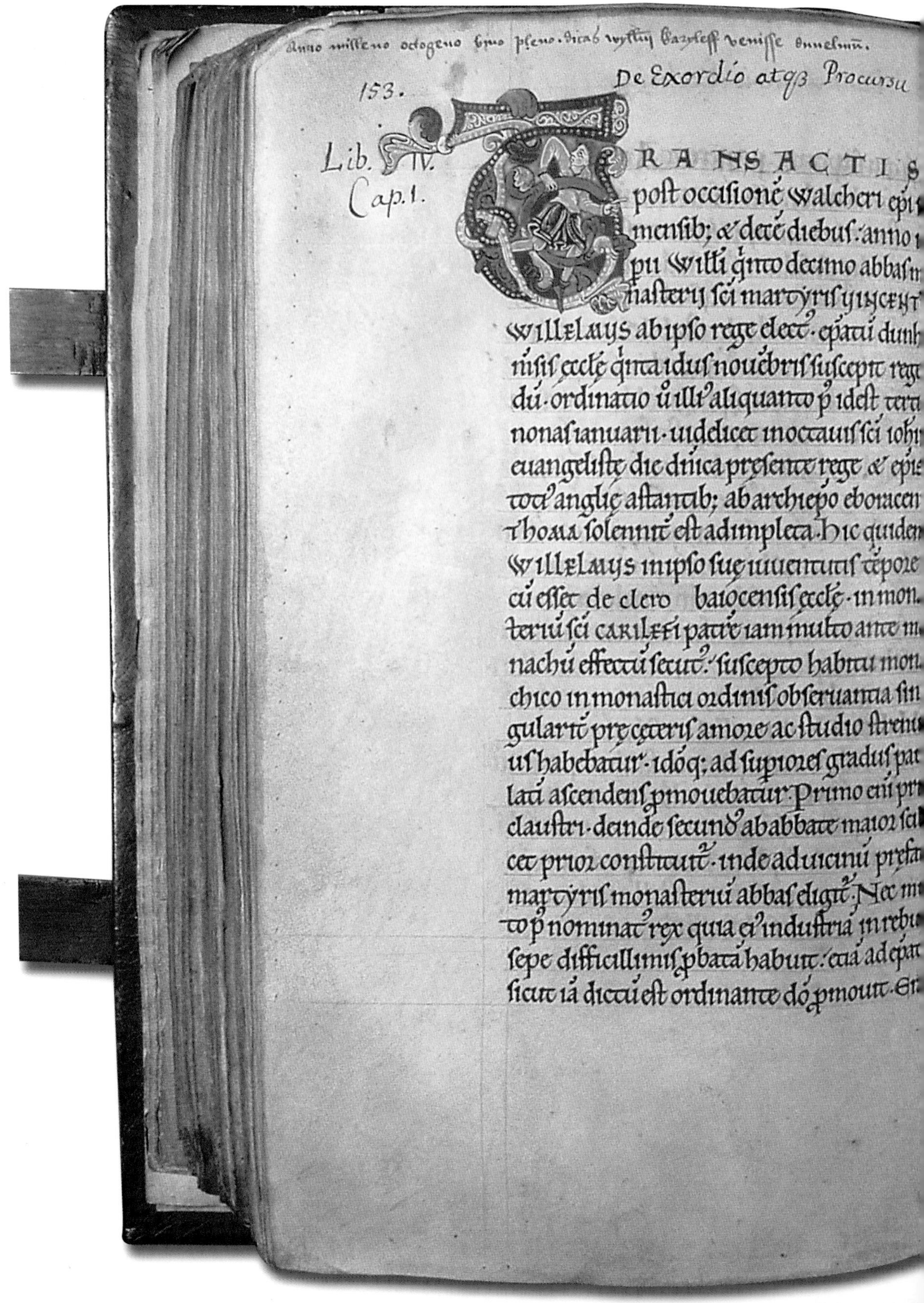

Anno milleno octogeno bino pleno. dicab wyllm Karylefi venisse dunelmu.

153.

De Exordio atq Procursu

Lib. IV.
Cap. I.

TRANSACTIS
post occisione walcheri epi
mensib; & dece diebus: anno
pii willi qinto decimo abbas m
nasterii sci martyris y incent
willelmus ab ipso rege elect. epatui dunh
nisis eccle qinta idus noue bris suscepit rege
du. ordinatio u illi aliquanto p idest tercio
nonas ianuarii. uidelicet in octauis sci iohi
euangeliste die dnica presente rege & epis
toci anglie astantib; ab archiepo eboracen
thoma solennit est adimpleta. Hic quidem
willelmus in ipso sue iuuentutis tepore
cu esset de clero baiocensis eccle. in mon
teriu sci carilefi patris iam multo ante m
nachu effectu secut: suscepto habitu mon
chico in monastici ordinis obseruantia sin
gulart pre ceteris amore ac studio strenu
us habebatur. ideoq; ad supiores gradus pa
lati ascendens p mouebatur. Primo eni pri
claustri. deinde secund ab abbate maior sci
cet prior constitut. inde ad uicinu prefa
martyris monasteriu abbas eligit. Nec m
to p nominat rex quia ei industria in rebu
sepe difficillimis p bata habuit: etia ad epa
sicut ia dictu est ordinante do p mouit. Er

Catalogue

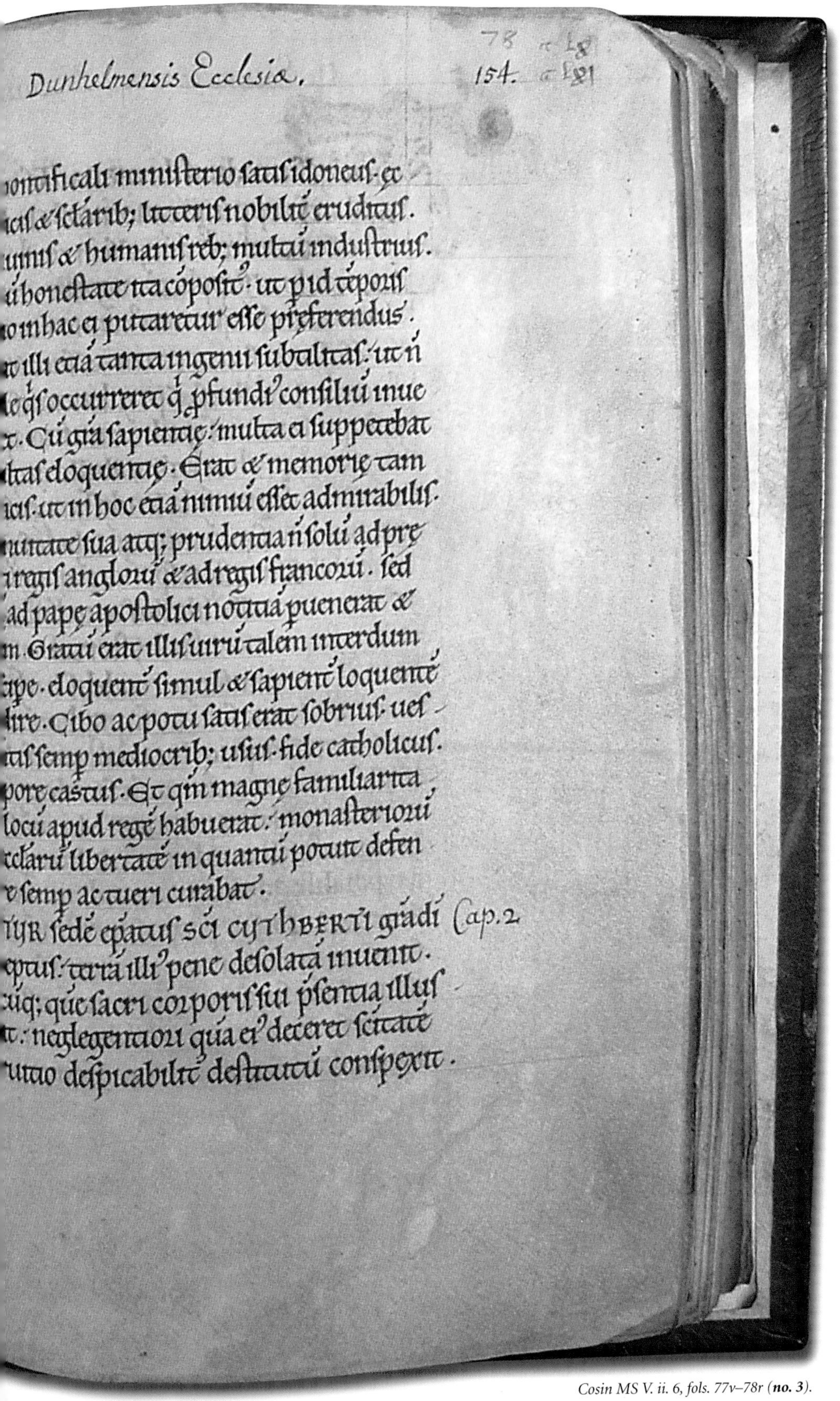

Cosin MS V. ii. 6, fols. 77v–78r (***no. 3***).

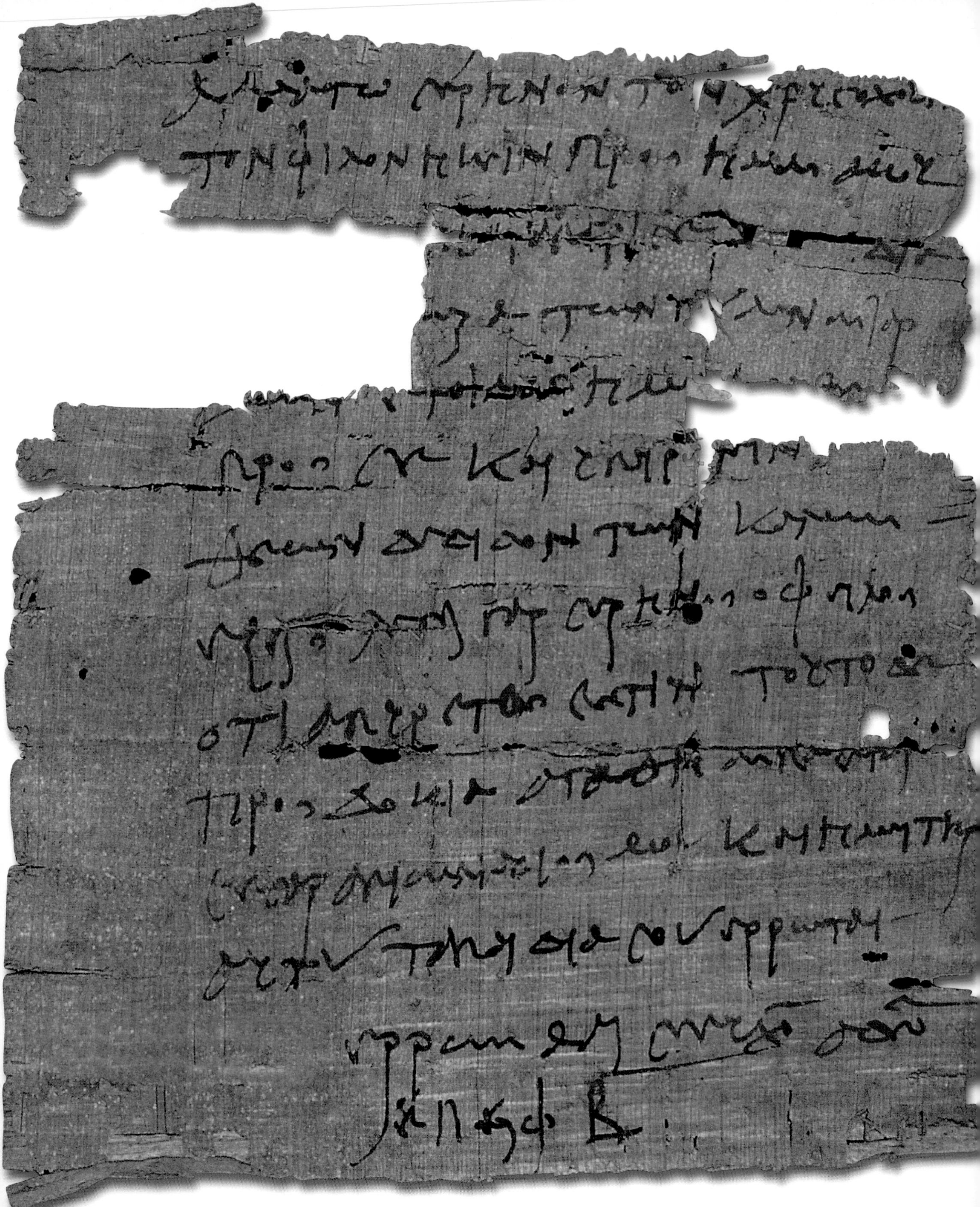

A Personal Letter from Roman Egypt

1

Single sheet of papyrus written in Egypt. 2nd century AD.

140 x 125 mm

Provenance: excavated at Oxyrhynchus, Egypt late 19th – early 20th century (P.Oxy.XII.1582). Given to Durham University Library *c.* 1920

OSR Cabinet B1

In the late nineteenth and early twentieth centuries B. P. Grenfell and A. S. Hunt excavated hundreds of papyri from Oxyrhynchus in Middle Egypt, on behalf of the Egypt Exploration Society. In the 1920s the Society distributed a number of papyri to various museums and libraries of institutions which had subscribed to the excavations; this text is one of three that it donated to Durham.

Papyrus was the commonest form of writing material in the Eastern Mediterranean until the arrival of paper in the early Middle Ages. Thanks to the dry climate, many thousands of papyri, in Egyptian, Greek, Latin and Arabic, have survived in the Egyptian sand (though not in the Nile Delta). Greek papyri from Oxyrhynchus vary greatly in content. Not much more than five per cent can be classed as literary: texts of Homer, the Greek tragedians, etc., centuries earlier than the surviving medieval manuscript copies; there are also a few early Christian writings, notably fragments of gospels, from the second and third centuries. The vast majority of texts are more ephemeral: official documents such as tax receipts, birth and death certificates, legal contracts of every kind, and private letters – one of which is shown here.

The papyrus is written in Greek, in a rapid cursive hand. It has no year date, but can be confidently assigned to the second century AD on the basis of the hand-writing. The black, carbon-based, ink still shows up very clearly.

The content is a private letter from Abascantus to Sarapion. Its unpretentious style is typical of papyrus letters at the time, in contrast to the more formal epistles known from Classical literature. It is almost complete, lacking only the first few lines. We do not know from where Abascantus was writing, but the recipient, Sarapion, was presumably living in Oxyrhynchus since this is where the letter was found. Abascantus addresses Sarapion as his brother, though this is no more than a general term of affection. He had heard that Sarapion had been taken ill and had been planning to come and look after him. However, with the arrival of another friend, Serenus, a goldsmith, he has had more encouraging news: 'If the gods grant, you will be well. For Serenus, our friend, says "he is free from fever". This means the expectation is good. Sarapion my son [clearly a different Sarapion from the addressee] and his mother send you their greetings. Your children are well.' The letter then ends with date (month and day only) and has an address on the back. It well illustrates the human interest of so many of the Greek papyri from Oxyrhynchus, which give us direct contact with people who lived two thousand years ago.

David Thomas

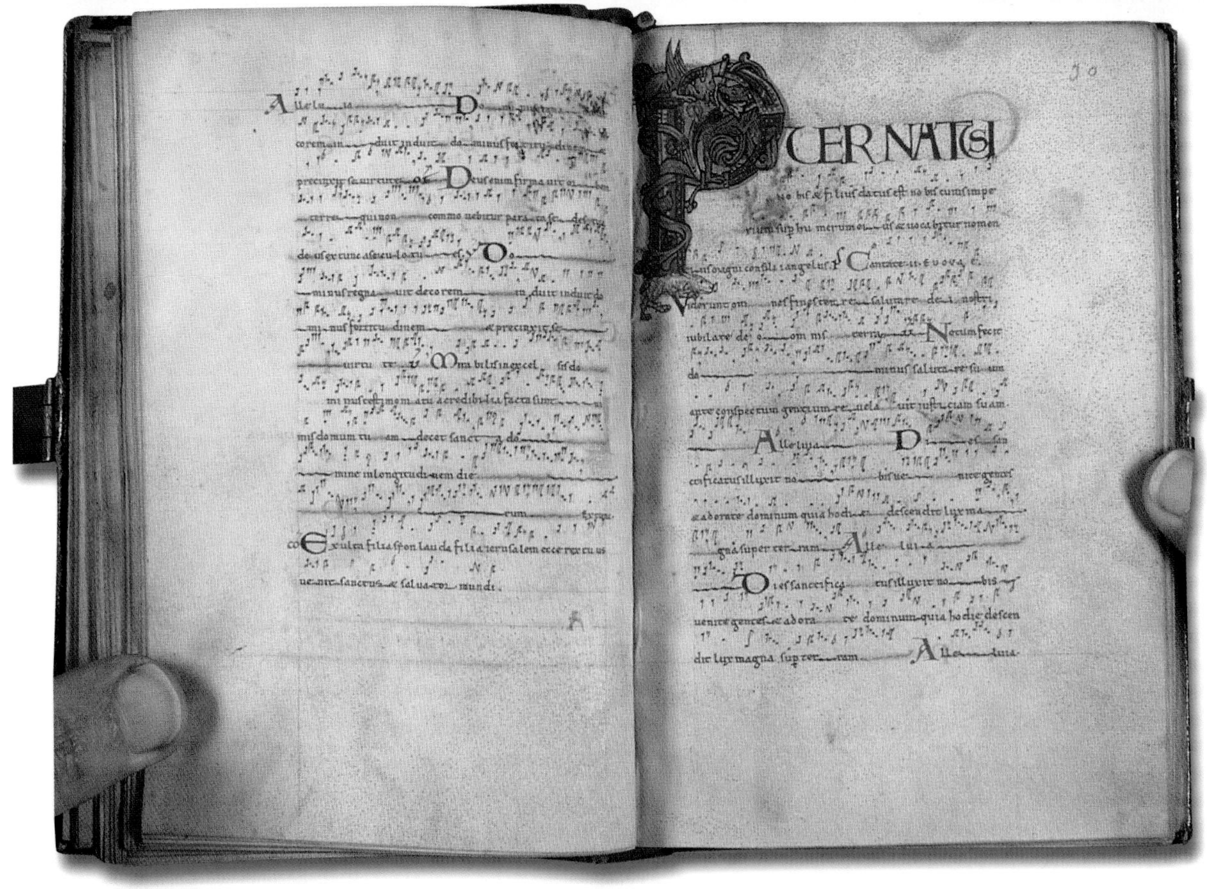
PUER NATUS

SPIRITUS DOMINI

The Divine Service in the Aftermath of the Norman Conquest

2

Benedictine gradual.

Parchment manuscript written at Canterbury, Christ Church Cathedral Priory in the late 11th century. [1]+1+128+[1] leaves. 160 x 65 mm (text-block: 110 x 65 mm).

Provenance: at Durham Cathedral Priory by ?1096; a number of late 16th- and early 17th-century names, most prominent Thomas Horsley (d. 1612), perhaps a recusant of Old Elvet, Durham; given to Cosin's Library by George Davenport.

Cosin MS V.v.6

A gradual contains the sung portions of the Mass, both 'ordinary' (i.e. unchanging, such as the *Kyrie* and *Gloria*) and 'proper' (varying according to the day or feast, such as introit, gradual, *Alleluia*, etc.). As this is the oldest surviving English example, its importance can hardly be overstated. Highly compact yet clear and comprehensive – designed to be conveniently portable for use by the precentor or succentor (the officials responsible for choral services) – it is a jewel of a book.

Texts in the core of the volume show that it was made at Christ Church, Canterbury: its *laudes regiae* (ruler acclamations) give greater prominence to the archbishop than the queen, omit bishops altogether, and highlight the Canterbury saints, Augustine, Dunstan (especially), and Ælphege. Equally, the elegant coloured capitals used throughout are of a distinctive form exclusive to Christ Church in the generation after the Norman Conquest; while the decorated initials (of which three survive) are akin to those in some coeval Christ Church books.

The original text is written on fine parchment in a minute yet legible hand using a script that owes more to Norman than to Anglo-Saxon traditions; the diastemic neums (staff-less musical notation) are equally of Anglo-Norman, rather than Anglo-Saxon, type: the appearance thus evokes the cultural changes that overtook England in the wake of the Norman Conquest. The political tensions of this process are illustrated locally by the circumstance that Durham's first Norman-appointed bishop, Walcher, was assassinated at Gateshead in May 1080, leading to a harrying of the North. His successor, William Carilef (1080/1–1096), transformed the cathedral into a Benedictine monastery (1083), and the present manuscript was probably acquired as part of his efforts to equip it: indeed, a contemporary list of the books that Carilef gave to his cathedral includes 'one gradual'. The wide-ranging content of our manuscript would suit it for such a role. (Several other 'core' texts seem also to have been acquired from Canterbury around this time, including copies of Archbishop Lanfranc's monastic Constitutions and his decretal collection.)

That our volume was indeed used in Durham from an early date is demonstrated by supplements added from *c.* 1100: the earliest stratum included Proses for the locally-culted saints, Aidan, Cuthbert and Oswald, along with one for St Vincent (patron saint of the abbey at Le Mans where Carilef had been abbot); further Proses for Cuthbert and Oswald were added in the later twelfth century. Subsequent additions, not to mention the re-working of some of the notation, show that the volume continued to see active service in the thirteenth and fourteenth centuries, possibly beyond.

Rendered obsolete by the Reformation, though happily not destroyed (the fate of most liturgical books: see no. 28), it was subsequently treated less reverently, as numerous informal jottings show. These include crude sketches of a man and a woman in Elizabethan garb (the former labelled 'T.H.'), written insults ('Antony Chaytor is a knave ...'), and an ex libris-cum-prayer in macaronic verse: Isti liber pertinit bere it well in mind / ad me Thomas Horslye bothe curtis and kind / A uinculo doloris Cryst him brynge ad / uitam eternam to the ever lasting king ('This book belongs, bear it well in mind, to me, Thomas Horslye, both courteous and kind. From the chain of sorrow, Christ him bring, to eternal life, to the everlasting king'). Presumably, then, the man in the sketch is Thomas Horslye.

To sum up: in addition to documenting the liturgy and music of Canterbury and Durham, and evoking the impact of the Norman Conquest, our gradual illustrates the high standards of certain scriptoria, the circulation of texts between distant centres, and the long working life that such a volume, clear, portable and practical, could enjoy.

Richard Gameson

An Authorial Romanesque Manuscript on the History of Durham

3

Symeon of Durham, *Tract on the Origins and Progress of this the Church of Durham.*

Parchment manuscript written at Durham between 1104 and 1115 with later 12th- and 16th-century additions. [1] + 8 + 87 + 10 + 11 + 1 + 4 + [1] leaves. 292 x 185 mm.

Provenance: Durham Cathedral Priory; passed through various local hands to John Cosin (recorded in catalogue of 1668).

Cosin MS V.ii.6

The main illustration shows the preface to the Durham monk Symeon's *Tract*, which concerns the churches not only of Durham (founded 995) but also of Lindisfarne (founded 635) and Chester-le-Street (founded 883) which Durham claimed as its predecessors. It includes an account of the replacement in 1083 of the Durham clerks with monks from the recently refounded monasteries of Monkwearmouth and Jarrow, and it finishes with the death of William Carilef, bishop of Durham 1080–96.

The text was copied contemporaneously with the composition of the *Tract* (1104 x 1107/1115), and it was corrected by the author Symeon himself. Some corrections involved erasure and sometimes supply of new text. Two thirds of the preface as originally written was erased, and Symeon supplied the present text in his own hand as a replacement. As noted in the margin by Thomas Rud (d. 1732), the name of Bishop Rannulf (see below) was also removed from the sixth line up. On folio 80, a passage seemingly concerning the expulsion of the Durham canons was erased but not replaced. This was evidently a sensitive matter, and no other copy of the work supplies what was suppressed; however, an account of how the canons were settled in the churches of Auckland, Darlington, Norton, and Easington occurs at this point in a late thirteenth- or fourteenth-century copy of the *Tract* now in York (Minster Library, MS XVI.I.12). Another erasure, for which no text is supplied by any other copy, may have concerned Durham's claim to the church of Carlisle; while the account of Tynemouth, a priory dependent on St Alban's by Symeon's time but once claimed by Durham, is significantly different in meaning in our manuscript from the parallel passage in a contemporary copy now in London (British Library, MS Cotton Faustina A. v).

Cosin V.ii.6 is thus crucial not only for the text of the *Tract*, but also for the processes by which a medieval history was corrected, altered and even expunged. Its text is the only one to include the list of early Durham monks, with a request for prayers for them, and it contains the earliest version of the Continuation which describes the career of Rannulf Flambard, bishop of Durham 1099–1128, including his kidnapping at sea and his escape from the Tower of London, the career of Bishop Geoffrey Rufus (1133–41), and the usurpation of the bishopric by William Cumin which ended with the installation of Bishop William of Ste Barbe (1143–52).

A description of Lindisfarne and a twelfth-century account of the trial of Bishop William Carilef were added in the sixteenth century, possibly by the Durham antiquary William Claxton (d. 1597), as were a couple of headings (one on the illustration).

David Rollason

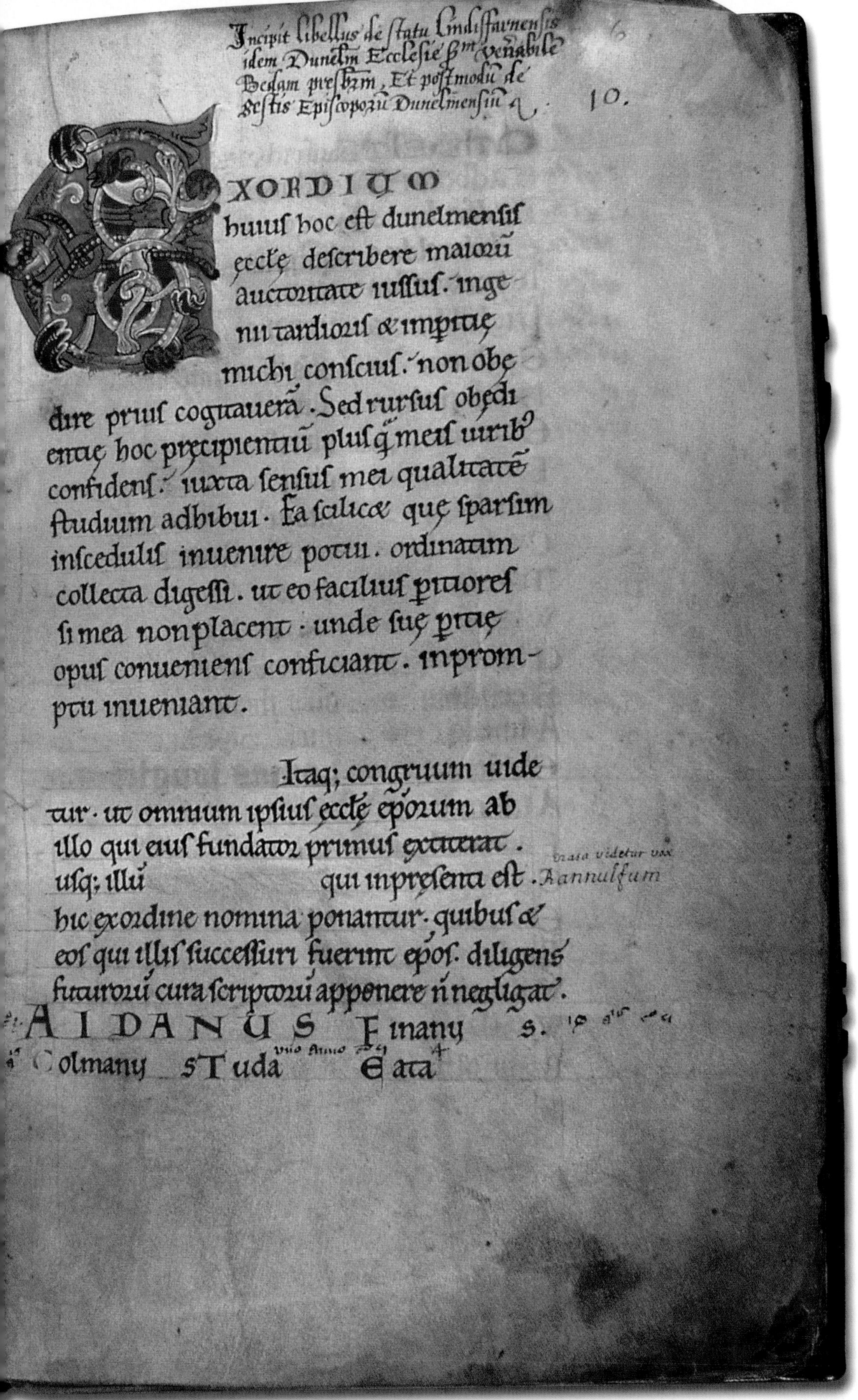

Incipit libellus de statu Lindisfarnensis idem Dunelm Ecclesie secundum venabilem Bedam presbiterum, Et postmodum de gestis Episcoporum Dunelmensium. 10.

EXORDIUM huius hoc est dunelmensis ecclesie describere maiorum auctoritate iussus. ingenii tardioris & imperitie michi conscius. non obedire prius cogitaueram. Sed rursus obedientie hoc precipientium plus quam meis uiribus confidens. iuxta sensus mei qualitatem studium adhibui. Ea scilicet que sparsim in scedulis inuenire potui. ordinatim collecta digessi. ut eo facilius peritiores si mea non placent. unde sue peritie opus conueniens conficiant. in promptu inueniant.

Itaque congruum uidetur. ut omnium ipsius ecclesie episcoporum ab illo qui eius fundator primus extiterat. usque illum qui in presentiarum est. *rasa videtur vox Rannulfum* hic ex ordine nomina ponantur. quibus & eos qui illis successuri fuerint episcopos. diligens futurorum cura scriptorum apponere non negligat.

AIDANUS Finanus Colmanus Tuda Eata

A Twelfth-Century Durham Play

4

Laurence of Durham, *Rithmus Laurencii de Christo et suis discipulis.* (fols. 104–106v)

Part of a collection of the Latin works of Laurence of Durham. Parchment manuscript probably written at Durham Cathedral Priory in the mid- to later 12th century. [1] + 1 + 1 + 107 + [1] leaves. 240 x 155 mm (text-block 190 x 100 mm).

Provenance: Durham Cathedral Priory; given to George Davenport in 1670 by Nicholas Freville (d. 1674).

Cosin MS V.iii.1

This collection of the Latin verse of Laurence, prior of Durham 1149–54, may have been completed shortly after his death; it is listed in 1395 and 1416 among the manuscripts kept in the cathedral spendement. On the first verso of two leaves added at the beginning is a list of contents; its first two items (Laurence's *Consolatio de morte amici* and his *Hypognosticon*) are in an unidentified fourteenth-century hand, the remainder in that of Thomas Swalwell (monk of Durham *c.* 1483–1539). Swalwell adds the titles of Laurence's five verse prayers and the *Rithmus*, but not the following *Prosa de Resurrectione*, which he may (probably correctly) have regarded as part of the *Rithmus*. The title of the *Rithmus* has also been inserted in pink before the beginning of its text, in a hand associated with William Claxton of Wynyard, Co. Durham (d. 1597).

This manuscript is usually noticed for its texts of Laurence's *Dialogues* (reflections on mortality and immortality arising from the turbulent historical circumstances at Durham in 1143–4) and *Hypognosticon* (a verse epic on the redemption of man's fallen nature), or for the tinted pen and ink drawing of Laurence – the earliest known portrait of a monk of Durham (see frontispiece). However, the relatively neglected last part of the manuscript is just as remarkable. It consists of a separate four-leaf quire, containing the *Rithmus* followed by the *Prosa de Resurrectione* – the only known copy of these works.

The *Rithmus* is a play in two scenes, the *Peregrinus* (The Pilgrims to Emmaus) and the Incredulity of Thomas (whose beginning is marked with an enlarged red initial). It has speaking parts (indicated in red in the left-hand margins) for two pilgrims to Emmaus, Christ, and ten named disciples, and is the only Anglo-Latin *Peregrinus* play that survives in full. It lacks liturgical context or stage directions (the latter presumably because its manuscript context is in a collection of verse, where liturgical rubrics were not required), but it may have been written for performance during Easter week, perhaps during Mass on Easter Monday. In structure it resembles the most developed Peregrinus plays from twelfth-century France – those from Beauvais and Fleury – which like Laurence's work include the Incredulity of Thomas, refer to Mary Magdalen but avoid introducing her as a character (presumably so that all roles could be male), and conclude with celebratory hymns that resemble Laurence's *Prosa de Resurrectione.* But unlike these Franco-Latin plays, Laurence's *Rithmus* is entirely in rhymed verse, whose metres are skilfully varied to reflect the play's structure. He also makes his characters convincingly different from each other; in the discussion between the two pilgrims, Cleophas is notably more pessimistic than his companion Lucas. Similarly, the disciples express a variety of attitudes to Mary Magdalen's testimony about the resurrection of Christ, while the words of Christ to the disciples and to Thomas are expressed in serene but strangely mysterious rhyming hexameters.

John McKinnell

Luca. Egra comes rerum mutatio. nos exponit erroz biuio.
nri ihu tam dulcis mutatio. nos meroris potat absinthio.
Cleoph. Hec est nre sortis conditio. crebro pulsans nos monitorio.
semp adest letis turbatio. spei metus. & dolor gaudio.
Luca. Ergo frat nra saluatio sic hebit in cursu medio. nec habe
bit fidem pmissio. facta nobis a dei filio.
Cleop. Cum spondente decessit sponsio. spes de uiuo pendet in du
bio. spes post mortem est deliratio. mors est omnis spei pcisio.
Luc. Sed marie iactat assertio. angelorum nitens indicio. quod reuixit
nra redemptio. cum qua spei fit reparatio.
Cleo. Digna certe xpi preconio. noue uite noua resumptio. pre
mit tamen fidem miratio. tardat metus. urget dilectio.
Luc. Mira tamen resuscitatio. boni ihu fit beneficio. dono cur non
usurus pro se surgat semel. suscitans tercio.
Cleo. Legem lege. non necessario surgit p quem fit resurrectio. Heli
seus arcens ab alio mortem cedit mortis imperio.
Luc. Premet g funeris modio tantum culmen tanta deiectio. nec sup est
spes in infortunio. nec claudetur dolor solatio.
Cleo. Dum laxamus frena colloquio nri fletus caret obsequio nri ihu
tam nra passio. fletus afficit non disputatio.
Xpc. Que sunt uba frs mei que deduxit dolor in medium. Suum
spent nutu dei uba fructum. dolor remedium.
Cleo. Tu solus o peregrine peregrinus es ierosolimis. nec scis rei tam uici
ne casum nris dicatum lacrimis.
Xpc. Que res. ul quis ordo rei. conuiantis decet indicium. restat enim
pars diei. restat uia. restat & otium.
Cleo. Vir uerendus. uir ppha. uir uirtutum. uir pstans ceteris. uir in quo
lex est impleta. potens ubi. potens & opis.
Hic ut semp in re leta res emergit diuersi generis. iuxta pnci
pum decreta ualescit occasus supis.
Iesus ingm nazarenus carus deo carus et poplo. dei xpc. deo plenus est af
fixus crucis patibulo.
Phariseum quippe genus debriatum liuoris poculo condempnatum
cruce tenus secli lumen extinxit seculo.
De uiro tam singulari sperabamus tam singularia. quod in illo restau
rari iactabamus dauid impia.
Sed euentus tam amari spem fefellit nram inuidia. quod flendo li
bet testari quam loquendo nouare testia.

tes uetes inuenimus uinu nouu. Uete
ra tn sient. ecce facta sunt omnia no
ua: p xpm dnm nrm cui e gla et imp
ium. in scla sclorum. am. Expl omel .x.

Incipit .xi. de eo qd scriptum est: sci
estote qa ego scs sum dicit dominus.

Nuper in auri
bus eccle recitatu
e. sermo dei dicens.
Sci estote: quia scs
sum dns ds ur. Ho
men hoc scm quid
sibi uelit. quid ue significet in scrip
turis diuinis diligentius reqrendu
e. ut cum illud nobis ds didicimus. etia
opus ei possim implere. Congregem
g de scripturis diuinis sup quibz scm
dici inuenim: et dep hendem n solu
homines sed etiam muta animalia
sca appellata. Inuenim et uasa mi
nistii sca uocitata. et uestimta sca di
ci: et loca nichilomin que in urbibz
ul sub urbibz posita sunt. et ea sacdo
tibz deputata. Ex multis quide ani
malibz pmogenita boum ul pecor
scificari p legem dno iubent. et dicit.
Ne facias inquit in eis opus ullu. qm
dno scificata sunt. Sup uasis u cu tab
naculo testimonii uasa ministii
thuribula. ul fiale. ul cta huiusmo
di uasa: sca appellant. Sup uestim
tis etiam cu stola pontificis aaron et
tunica linea: et cta huiusmodi uesti
menta sca dicunt. Si g inueniam q sen
su hec omnia sca nominata st: addi
cem quom etia nos dare opam debea
mus. ut sci ee possim. Natus e m pmo
genitus bos: non m licet occupare eu
ad opus comune. Est eni dno consecr:
et ideo dicit scs. Intelligim g ex hoc mu

to animali. quom lex qd scm u
nulli alii id deseruire iubet. n
li. Sicum patere ul fiale qs dicit sc
sunt que nunqm exire iubent
plo. sed ee semp in scis. nec ulli p
humanis usibz ministrare. Si
et uestimta que sca nominant
tur int domu usui deseruire p
tis: sed in templo ee. et inde om
nunqm efferri: sed ad hoc tantu
cta ee. ut is deo ministris pontif
duantur: et sint semp in templo.
os u usus comunes: utant comun
duntas. Similit et patenis ac fial
que sca appellant: ad humanos c
munes usus uti n licet: sed tantu
uina ministia. Qd si intellectu
ul animalia. ul uas ul uestim
pellat: consequent intellige qd h
nationibz et legibz etia homo sca
tur. Siquis eni se xpm deuouit de
nullis negotiis sclaribz se implicat
ei placeat cui se pbauit: siquis se
et segregat a reliquis hominibz ca
t uiuentibz. et mundanis negotii
gant: non querens ea que terram. sed
in celis scis sunt: iste mito scs appell
Donec eni pmixtus e turbis et inm
tudine fluctuantiu uolutat: nec u
soli deo segregat a uulgo: n potest
Nam de his quid dicemus qui cum g
aliis turb ad spectacula manant
spectis suos atq; audit impudicis
et actibz fedant: Non e nrm pm
de talibz. Ipsi eni senitre et uide pos
sibi deleginit partem. Ii g qui hec au
cui hec diuina recitant: quie ipsius
dei sermo conuenit dicens. sci estote
et ego scs sum dns ds ur. sapient m
ge que dicunt: ut sis beat cum fili

A Majestic Manuscript of Origen

5

Origen, *Homiliae in Vetere Testamento.*

Parchment manuscript written in England in the second half of the 12th century. [1] + 2 + 203 + 2 + [1] leaves. 420 x 290 mm.

Provenance: given to Cosin's Library by George Davenport, 1670.

Cosin MS V.i.1

This imposing volume contains Latin translations of most of Origen's homilies on the Old Testament. Origen (*c.* 185–*c.* 254) was one of the greatest – and certainly the most prolific and influential – exegetes of the early church. The son of Christian parents (though perhaps not Christians then: his name means 'son of Horus'), he was born in Alexandria. His father died in the persecution of Christians in Alexandria in 202, and Origen would have followed him, had his mother not prevented his going out by hiding his clothes! After the persecution, Origen was, despite his youth, appointed head of the catechetical school in Alexandria. During this time, he sought to learn what he could about Greek philosophy, and became a student of Ammonios Sakkas (who may also have been the mentor of the great third-century philosopher, Plotinos). He grew so famous that at one point he was summoned to speak to Julia Mamaea, the mother of the Emperor Alexander Severus (ruled 222–35). Around 230, Origen fell out with his bishop, and settled in Caesarea, where he established a school of theology; many of his pupils became distinguished bishops. In the persecution of Christians ordered by the Emperor Decius (250–1), he was tortured in the hope of breaking his will; he survived the persecution only to die of his wounds in 253/4.

Central to Origen's scholarly work was the interpretation of the Bible; he is reputed to have written and preached on virtually the whole of the Christian Scriptures. He was also a speculative theologian, and his speculations – about the origin of human kind and its ultimate destiny – attracted criticism both in his time and after. He was formally condemned by various church synods, especially the Fifth Œcumenical Synod of 553, and thereafter, relatively few of his works were preserved in the original Greek. In the fourth century, however, Origen had been a principal resource for biblical exegetes, and Rufinus of Aquileia (*c.* 345–411) translated many of his works into Latin, notably most of his Old Testament homilies (not the more controversial and scholarly commentaries, though he translated Origen's vast commentary on Paul's Epistle to the Romans). The bulk of this is in our volume: translations of the homilies on Genesis (including a homily on the benedictions of the Patriarchs [Gen. 49] by Rufinus himself), Exodus, Leviticus (the very beautiful homilies on Numbers, the last to be translated by Rufinus, are missing), Joshua, Judges, Kings, Isaiah, Jeremiah and Ezekiel. Durham Cathedral Priory had acquired a very similar collection by 1096, and this remains in the cathedral library (MS B.III.1). The origin of the present manuscript is unknown, though it has the hallmarks of a monastic reading book, with hints of Cistercian affiliations; certainly, in their efforts to draw on ancient Christian tradition, the Cistercians, not least Bernard of Clairvaux, used Origen's homilies as translated by Rufinus.

Andrew Louth

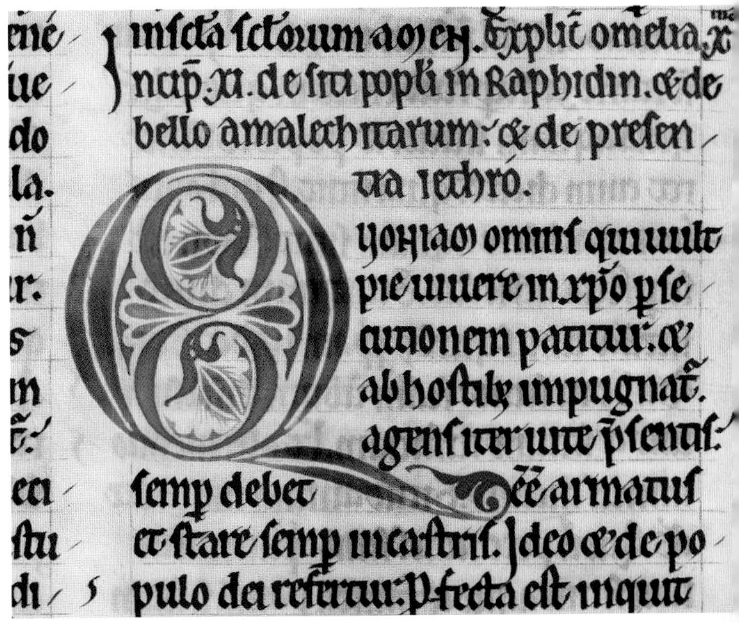

eius oleo. quē unxit ds p̄ oleo letitie p̄ consortibꝫ suis. Pfundimini & uos oleo mīe & pietatis. n̄ ematis olim peccatoris. n̄ ab exprobrantibꝫ sic fatue uirgines mutuo petatis. sꝫ abundantes tribuite. & tribuentes abundate. ut qđ minus habetis in lauacro & in uestibꝫ. unctionis sacre copia restauretur. Et quoniam olei talis natura est. ut omībꝫ liquoribꝫ quibꝫ fuit iniectum superferatur. de hoc oleo spirituali sentiatis qđ scriptum est. miserationes dni super omīa opera eius. ut sic coronati in misericordia & miserationibꝫ. ad ipsum feliciter ueniatis. qui cum patre & spiritu sancto uiuit & regnat deus. per infinita secula amen. Sermo de ael. ab. de Rie

xix

Satis nouit di in ascensione lectio ura fres kmi. dominus quemadmodum imperator noster ab illo solio glorie sue. ab illo palatio diuinitatis sue. ab illo insuper secreto patris simus uenit in hunc mundum saluare qđ perierat. captiuos redimere. patriam quam callidus hostis inuaserat. suis iterum legibꝫ subiugare. Ecce. factum est qđ intendit. Debellauit aduersarium. afflixit inimicum. eripuit inopem de manu fortioris eius. egenum & pauperem a diripientibꝫ eum. Absoluit captiuos. patriam fugato hoste recepit. Omnibꝫ itaqꝫ pro uoto peractis. hodie cum uictoribꝫ signis suam ingreditur ciuitatem. a ciuibꝫ suis cum ineffabili iocunditate recipitur. Inde est ista festiuitas. inde per uniuersum orbem tanta letitia hominibꝫ immittitur. pro suo modulo illi angelice processioni gaudia imitantibꝫ. & qui possunt deuotione & affectu dominum suum ad celestia ascendentem prosequentibꝫ. Tota utique celestis curia prodit obuiam. & diu desideratum suum hodie recipiunt imperatorem. Ipse insuper pater suum alloquitur filium quem solabundus. sede inquiens a dextris meis. donec ponam inimicos tuos scabellum pedibꝫ tuis. Iste est enim uerus ille iacob. qui primum fit in mesopotamiam mundi huius. duxit ibi ducturum uxorem. ecclesiam scilicet de iudeis & gentibꝫ. Et pauper quidem mesopotamiam ingreditur. sꝫ admodum diues & locupletatus egreditur. In baculo inquit meo transiui iordanem istum. & nunc cum duabꝫ turmis regredior. Pauper quidem uenit in mundum. Pauper plane. adeo. ut non esset ei locus in diuersorio. & ideo natus reclinatur in presepio. Vulpes foueas habent. & uolucres celi nidos. filius autem hominis. non habet ubi caput reclinet. In baculo meo inquit transiui iordanem istum. Quem iordanem. Istum utique istum. Iordanis interpretatur descensus. illi nimirum ut casum exprimens ut descensum. qui descendit ab ierusalem in iericho. & incidit in latrones. O miserabilis descensus. Descendit quippe miser ille adam de uita ad mortem. de securitate ad timorem. de incorruptione ad corruptionem. de ierusalem in iericho. O infelix adam. quid tibi et iericho. Nonne in ierusalem idest in paradiso ubi habitas pacata sunt omnia. omnia sana. omnia iocunda. Quid queris in iericho. Ierusalem interpretatur uisio pacis. Sic pacis. Pax tibi o adam in eternitate. in ueritate. in caritate. Caritas

Pax
- eternitatis
- ueritatis
- caritatis

natura / ratione / uoluntate

A Northern Monastic Sermon Collection

6

Ailred of Rievaulx and Achard of Saint-Victor, *Sermones.*

Parchment manuscript written in England at the end of the 12th or start of the 13th century (after 1167). [1] + 3 + 75 + 1 + 18 + [1] leaves. 300 x 220 mm.

Provenance: presumably written at or near a Cistercian house, possibly Rievaulx; inscriptions in the text include one from East Yorkshire; given to George Davenport by Timothy Thurscross, a canon of York 1622–71 and vicar of a parish near to Rievaulx in succession to his father.

Cosin MS V.i.11

Two notable English authors of the mid-twelfth century are represented in this functional and much-used manuscript, an important witness for the works it contains. Sermons by Ailred of Rievaulx form the bulk of the contents, the majority copied by a single scribe, with a second adding a sermon on the assumption of the Virgin Mary. A third hand was responsible for a sermon by Achard of Saint-Victor which follows. A probable connection with a Cistercian house of northern England adds to the importance of the manuscript as an early local witness not only to Ailred, but also Achard who may have spent some of his early life within the community at Bridlington, Yorkshire.

Ailred of Rievaulx is a familiar figure in the history of monastic life in England, of the Cistercian Order, and of theological writing in the twelfth century. A member of the Scottish royal court under David I, Ailred enthusiastically adopted Cistercian life in 1134, becoming Abbot of Rievaulx in 1147. Beloved of his community – his last years are chronicled movingly by Walter Daniel – Ailred died in 1167. Particularly famous for his extended discussions of spiritual friendship and the close analysis of a theology of love characteristic of early Cistercian writers, Ailred also composed a significant corpus of sermons, including a series on Isaiah and others for feasts throughout the liturgical year. Apart from the Isaiah set, Ailred seems not to have edited his sermons personally, a fact which underlines the importance of collections such as that represented here. Some twenty-six sermons, as well as that on the assumption of the Virgin, are included in this manuscript. The feasts appropriate to the sermons are indicated in the headings, running-titles, or side-notes. In his sermons Ailred uses the full techniques of interpretation according to the four senses of scripture, from the literal to the allegorical; the theme of love or charity is ever-present.

Achard was born around the beginning of the twelfth century, probably in England, where his early monastic life may have included time at Bridlington. The details of his association with the abbey of Saint-Victor are hazy until 1155, the occasion of his election as abbot. Appointed as bishop of Sées in 1157, but never installed, he became bishop of Avranches (Normandy) in 1161, a position he held until his death in 1170. An association with Saint-Victor in the mid-twelfth century places Achard at the heart of the developing scholastic community in Paris, and his intellectual style has been linked to the Victorine tradition – that is, moving seamlessly between scriptural exegesis and a more philosophical approach to his material. However, the corpus of Achard's surviving works is not large: some fifteen sermons and two treatises. The sermon included in Cosin V.i.11 (by convention, 'no. 15') enjoyed wider circulation than most of his works. It is a long homily for Lent comprising a discussion of Jesus being led into the desert by the Spirit, and taking the form of a spiritual journey through seven deserts, each leading to a more intense experience of God; it is dominated by a lengthy discussion of the respective roles of faith and reason.

Giles Gasper

A Fine Psalter from Scotland

7

Latin Psalter.

Parchment manuscript written
in Britain *c.* 1200. 122 leaves. 298 x 205 mm.

Provenance: probably written for Holyrood Abbey, Scotland. Given to St Michael le Belfrey in York by Percival Crawfurth. Probably acquired by one of the members of the Sharp family who held high ecclesiastical office in the northern province in the 18th century, when it joined the family library at Bamburgh Castle.

Bamburgh Select 6

This handsome manuscript contains the psalms, followed by canticles and prayers, and preceded by a calendar. Beautifully written in a bold, early Gothic formal book-hand, seemingly by a single scribe, the main text is articulated by a hierarchy of ornament. Each verse is headed by a coloured initial, each psalm by a larger golden letter with penwork flourishing. Still grander decorated initials highlight Psalms 1, 26, 38, 51, 52, 68, 80, 97, 101 and 109 – a common sequence conflating the eight-fold division for liturgical use (1, 26, 38, 68, 80, 97, 109) with a tripartite division (1, 51, 101) – that for Psalm 1, the start of the text and common to both systems, being the largest and most elaborate. The decorative repertoire, which includes dragons, spirals, sprigs and beast-masks, along with little lions, was widely current from the later twelfth century in England and, above all, northern France, and is accordingly known as the 'Channel style'. The specimens in our book are distinguished by the elongation of some of the beast-masks, the little hoods that a couple of them wear, and by a pair of crested, beaked avian heads. That the scribe and illuminator were distinct is seemingly confirmed by the malcoordination of their work at the very beginning of the Psalter. The former began writing at the fourth word of Psalm 1 ('non'); however, this was also supplied as the last word of the coloured lettering accompanying the initial – so the scribe's version was then erased.

The date of *c.* 1200 suggested by script and decoration is broadly confirmed by the integral graded calendar, which includes the feast of Thomas Becket in December as an original entry, while that of his translation in July was an early addition – indicating production between 1173 and 1220.

Distinctive feasts given prominence in the calendar suggest that the book was prepared for use by a house of Augustinian canons, in Scotland, with a particular devotion to the Cross – probably, therefore, Holyrood, a foundation endowed by King David I of Scotland between 1128 and 36. Whether it was written there, however, is debatable, for by 1200 professional ateliers were playing an increasingly important role in book production, and its script and decoration have as much in common with known products of such workshops as with the dwindling numbers of volumes whose manufacture can be certainly assigned to religious communities. The one other psalter of Scottish provenance to which our manuscript is comparable (the early thirteenth-century 'Iona Psalter', now in Edinburgh, NLS 10,000) was seemingly made in Oxford for 'export' to the newly-founded Augustinian nunnery on Iona.

Our manuscript had a long working life, as additions and alterations attest. First, titles were squeezed in before each psalm; then, still in the thirteenth century, various additions were made to the calendar – including the translation of Becket (1220), an obit for King David, and the 'Dedication of the church of Glasgow'. In the early fourteenth century, prayers for use before and after the psalter were prefixed to the book, which was probably rebound around the same time. In the fifteenth century, the first six months of the calendar were augmented with sigla for charting moveable feasts, complemented by a nineteen-year table. Whether the book remained at Holyrood all this time is unclear – the tumultuous history of that house in the later Middle Ages (sacked then nearly burned by the English in 1322 and 1385 respectively), allied to the added reference to the church of Glasgow, might suggest it had moved elsewhere (possibly Blantyre, an Augustinian house dedicated to Holy Cross in the diocese of Glasgow).

Holyrood was sacked yet again in 1544 and 1547 – by which time our manuscript was certainly in English hands. The first reference to Becket in the calendar was (imperfectly) expunged (as required by Henry VIII's legislation of 1538), and all occurrences of the word 'Pope' were crossed out; at the end of the book, the prayers

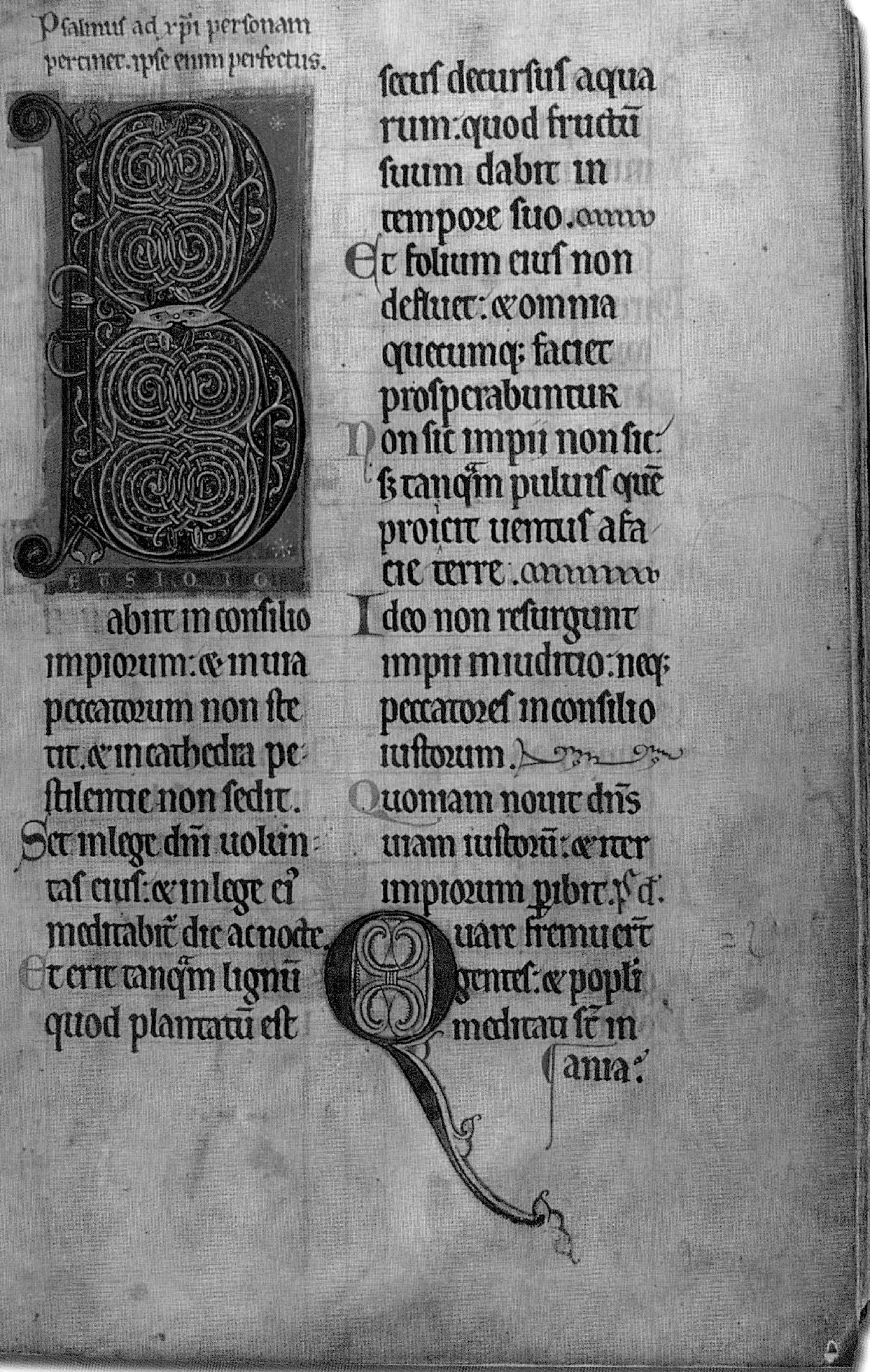

Psalmus ad xp̄i personam
pertinet. ipse enim perfectus.

Beatus uir qui non
abiit in consilio
impiorum: et in uia
peccatorum non ste
tit. et in cathedra pe
stilentie non sedit.
Sed in lege dn̄i uolun
tas eius: et in lege ei'
meditabit' die ac nocte.
Et erit tanq̄m lignū
quod plantatū est

secus decursus aqua
rum: quod fructū
suum dabit in
tempore suo.
Et folium eius non
defluet: et omnia
quecumq; faciet
prosperabuntur.
Non sic impii non sic:
s; tanq̄m puluis quē
proicit uentus a fa
cie terre.
Ideo non resurgunt
impii in iudicio: neq;
peccatores in consilio
iustorum.
Quoniam nouit dn̄s
uiam iustorū: et iter
impiorum peribit. Ps d.
Quare fremuerūt
gentes: et popli
meditati sūt in
ania.

to the cross were laboriously deleted, and other 'suspect' devotions thereafter may simply have been excised. Such purging is common to liturgical books that were in England in the mid-sixteenth century. More remarkable is the provision here of new numbering (following 'protestant' rather than Vulgate usage) along with liturgical notes, indicating the use for Matins or Vespers for most of the thirty-day cycle as appointed in the Book of Common Prayer (1549). The provenance of the manuscript around this time is documented by a florid inscription at the front, recording that on 22 August 1558 it was given to the church of St Michael le Belfrey in York by Percival Crawfurth – who three years later became mayor of that city (see p.157).

In sum, this elegant psalter, with its rare Scottish medieval provenance, continued in use throughout the sixteenth century. A reminder of how long after the invention of movable type, medieval manuscripts remained an active – as opposed to 'antiquarian' – part of book culture, it is also a graphic witness to both the changes and the continuities of the English Reformation.

Richard Gameson

8

Royal Marriage in a Gothic Pontifical

Pontifical (noted).

Parchment manuscript written in northern France in the first third of the 13th century. [1] + 103 + [1] leaves. Size: 214x144 mm (text-block 141 x 88 mm).

Provenance: possibly brought from France to Canterbury in the late 13th or early 14th century; belonged to Thomas Cranmer, archbishop of Canterbury (d. 1556); entered in 1668 Cosin Library catalogue.

Cosin MS V.iii.13

A pontifical contains the texts of rites proper to a bishop. The present copy begins with a cycle of episcopal blessings for use at Mass, in accordance with the liturgical year (from Christmas to around All Saints), followed by *ordines* for blessing a church and its components (the start of which is reproduced opposite); then, after the Canon of the Mass, comes a sequence of rites for consecrating officers of the church, culminating in services for blessing first a king and finally the nuptials of a queen.

Of compact size, well-written by a small team of scribes, its many subdivisions clearly signalled by a hierarchy of red and blue pen-flourished initials, most of the chants accompanied by bold notation on a four-line staff, our manuscript was manifestly designed as a practical 'working' copy. The formula for the consecration of a bishop implies that the core of the book was destined for use within the archdiocese of Reims; a northern French origin is further indicated by the choice of blessings in the liturgical cycle which is most closely paralleled in books from that region. Though the initial stratum was not quite brought to completion – some rubrics, notation and the end of the final text were not supplied, while texts for certain standard occasions are lacking – extensive supplements (in the margins and at the end, making good some of the deficiencies) show that it saw continuing use during and beyond the thirteenth century.

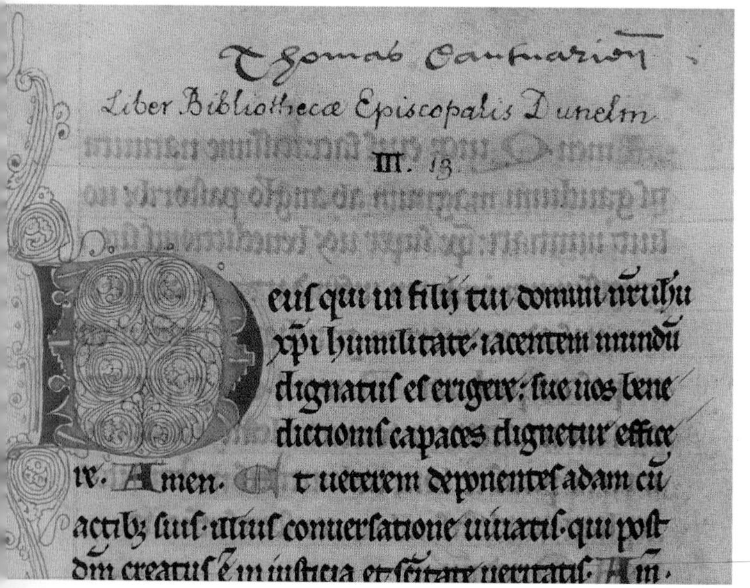

Particularly notable is the section for the nuptials of a queen with which the original stratum terminates. Amidst many fairly standard formulae, those texts most specifically relevant for the occasion stress the indissoluble nature of marriage (the gospel reading is Matthew 19, 3–11, '... what God has joined together, let no man put asunder…') and articulate the qualities of a model wife: 'may hers be a union of love and peace; may she be faithful and chaste, married in Christ'; 'may she be a steadfast imitator of holy women'; 'may she be amiable to her husband as was Rachel, wise as was Rebecca, long-lived and faithful as was Sarah…'; 'may she be great with modesty, venerable with decency, learned in sacred doctrine; may she be fruitful in offspring…'. Whilst doubtless providing a fair reflection of the ideal queen – indeed matron – of the thirteenth century, these texts (like most liturgical ones) had a long lineage: all the elements quoted above can be traced back to the ninth-century coronation *ordo* of Queen Ermentrude, first wife of the Frankish king Charles the Bald. Yet in the wake of the protracted dispute between Philip Augustus (king of France 1180–1223) and his second wife, Ingeborg of Denmark (d. 1238) – whose marriage in August 1193 was annulled in November that year but finally revalidated twenty years later – such words are likely to have been particularly resonant.

Incipit ordo ad benedicendam ecclesiam. Primum ueniat episcopus indutus uestimentis suis similiter et clerus ad eum locum in quo sanctorum reliquie preterita nocte cum uigiliis fuerunt. ibique fiat confessio et dicantur cum oratione ista preces.

Actiones nostras quesumus domine et aspirando preueni et adiuuando prosequere: ut cuncta nostra operatio atque locutio et a te semper incipiat: et per te cepta finiatur. Per.

Exorcizo te creatura salis per deum uiuum. per deum uerum. per deum sanctum. per deum qui te per heliseum prophetam in aquam mitti iussit. ut sanaretur sterilitas aque: ut efficiaris sal exorcizatum in salutem credentium. et sis omnibus te sumentibus sanitas anime et corporis: ut effugiat atque discedat ab eo loco quo aspersus fueris. omnis fantasia et nequitia uel uersutia diabolice fraudis omnisque spiritus inmundus. adiuratus per eum qui uenturus est iudicare uiuos et mortuos et seculum per ignem. Amen.

Immensam clementiam tuam

Since royalty were generally married before they came to the throne, the number of occasions on which nuptial blessings for a queen could be used was limited. There were only a couple of opportunities in France during the thirteenth century: the marriage of Marguerite of Provence to Louis IX in 1234, and that of Mary of Brabant to Philip III in 1274. Whether our manuscript was actually borne by one of the episcopal participants at these occasions – as opposed to merely transmitting the *ordo* as part of its 'package' of texts – is debatable: it is probably old enough to have been used at both of them, but the unfinished nature of the relevant section hardly favours usage.

By the sixteenth century, if not before, the manuscript had crossed the Channel and belonged to Thomas Cranmer, archbishop of Canterbury 1533–55 – as is shown by the inscription, 'Thomas Cantuariensis', that was added to the first page by the hand that labelled most of his books thus. Cranmer's personal library was, by the standards of his day, a large one, from which some 600 printed books and sixty to seventy manuscripts can still be identified. Yet hardly any of them are liturgical: the fact that our manuscript is virtually the only true service book that can certainly be associated with Cranmer, architect of the Anglican liturgy, adds materially to its interest; and it is impossible not to wonder what this veteran of Henry VIII's reign, caught up in the king's turbulent marital politics, would have thought upon reading the texts for sanctifying royal marriage.

Richard Gameson

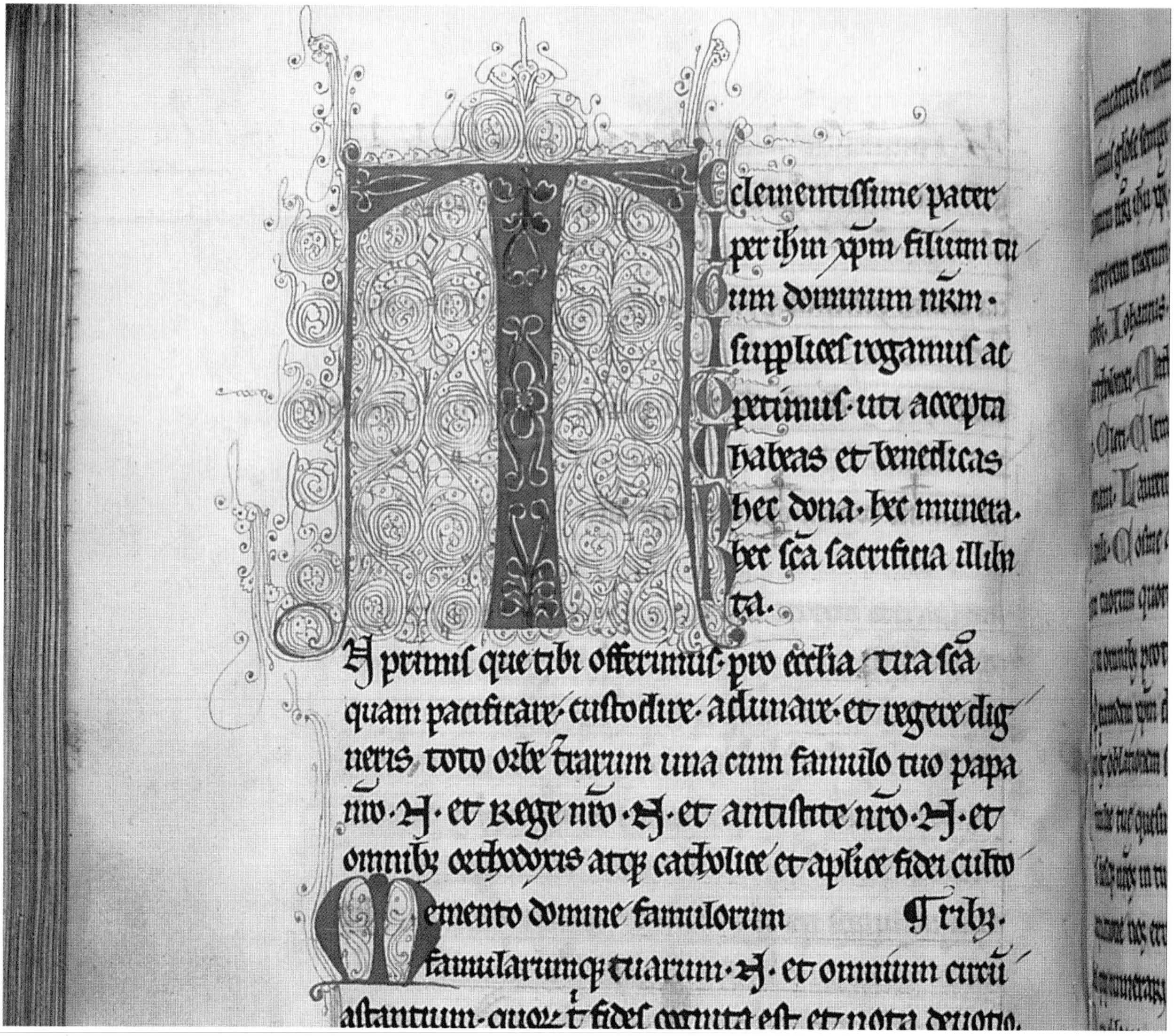

Eterne deus: Et te in ueneratione beate marie semper uirginis exultantibus animis collaudare. benedicere et predicare. Que et unigenitum tuum sancti spiritus obumbratione concepit: et uirginitatis gloria permanente huic mundo lumen eternum effudit: ihesum christum dominum nostrum. Per quem.

Equum et salutare. Te domine suppliciter exorare: ut gregem tuum pastor eterne non deseras: sed per beatos apostolos tuos continua protectione custodias. Ut eisdem rectoribus gubernetur: quos operis tui uicarios eidem contulisti preesse pastores. Et ideo.

PER OMNIA secula seculorum. Amen.

Dominus uobiscum. Et cum spiritu tuo. Sursum corda. Habemus ad dominum. Gratias agamus domino deo nostro. Dignum et iustum est.

A Thirteenth-Century Pocket-Bible

9

Biblia vulgata.

Parchment manuscript written in France in the mid-13th century.
[1] + 3 + 320 + [1] leaves. 128 x 93 mm.

Provenance: note on fol. 2 says that King James IV of Scotland (d. 1513) left this book to the chief of the Ogilvy family, the earls of Airlie; it was then given to Professor David Dickson of Edinburgh and to John Hall of Durham; James Mickleton gave it to George Davenport in 1669.

Cosin MS V.v.17

This small Latin Vulgate Bible – the main text supplemented by an (incomplete) list of Hebrew names with their meanings – is written in a script so tiny as to be barely legible to the naked eye. On the other hand, the subdivisions within the manuscript are clearly signalled by a hierarchy of decorated initials. Whereas eleventh- and twelfth-century Latin Bibles were generally massive volumes for communal use, in the thirteenth century, reflecting the growth in the numbers of individual readers (above all in the emerging universities), smaller formats were pioneered. Equally, the order of the biblical books was standardized and the new (familiar) subdivisions introduced (the Acts of the Apostles had been allotted a variety of positions; here it is placed between the Pauline and the Catholic Epistles, as was conventional in thirteenth-century French Bibles). While Paris was unquestionably the epicentre for the production of such Bibles, others places soon imitated the new format, as the present example shows.

The so-called 'Vulgate' (i.e. common) Bible was prepared by the great fourth-century saint and scholar, Jerome, at the behest of Pope Damasus (366–84). It was intended to replace the older Latin versions of the Scriptures, collectively referred to as the 'Old Latin', *Vetus Latina.* In the case of the Old Testament, Jerome's intention was to replace the Old Latin translation of the Greek Septuagint with a translation of the Hebrew Bible. This was only partially achieved. Frequently his text was a revision that preserved much of the (by-then-traditional) Septuagint text, rather than a fresh translation from the Hebrew; in the case of the Psalms he produced two texts, a revision based on the Septuagint (the 'Gallican' psalter) and one based on the Hebrew text, but it was the former that became standard. Jerome's enthusiasm for 'Hebrew truth' (*Hebraica veritas*) was not universally shared. The legend (found in the Letter to Aristeas) of the miraculous production of the Septuagintal text by the seventy (or seventy-two) translators, after whom it was known, carried great weight among Christians; the Septuagintal version was regarded as at least as authoritative as the Hebrew version. Augustine engaged in correspondence with Jerome over his translation, and maintained that the Septuagintal translators were to be regarded as inspired prophets themselves, as well as translators (cf. *The City of God* XVIII, 43). It was only gradually that the Vulgate established itself in the Latin West, one of the first to use this revised and more accurate version being Bede of Jarrow. The appendix of Hebrew names bears witness to the importance attached to the meaning of names, both in the Scriptures and in subsequent Christian interpretation.

Andrew Louth

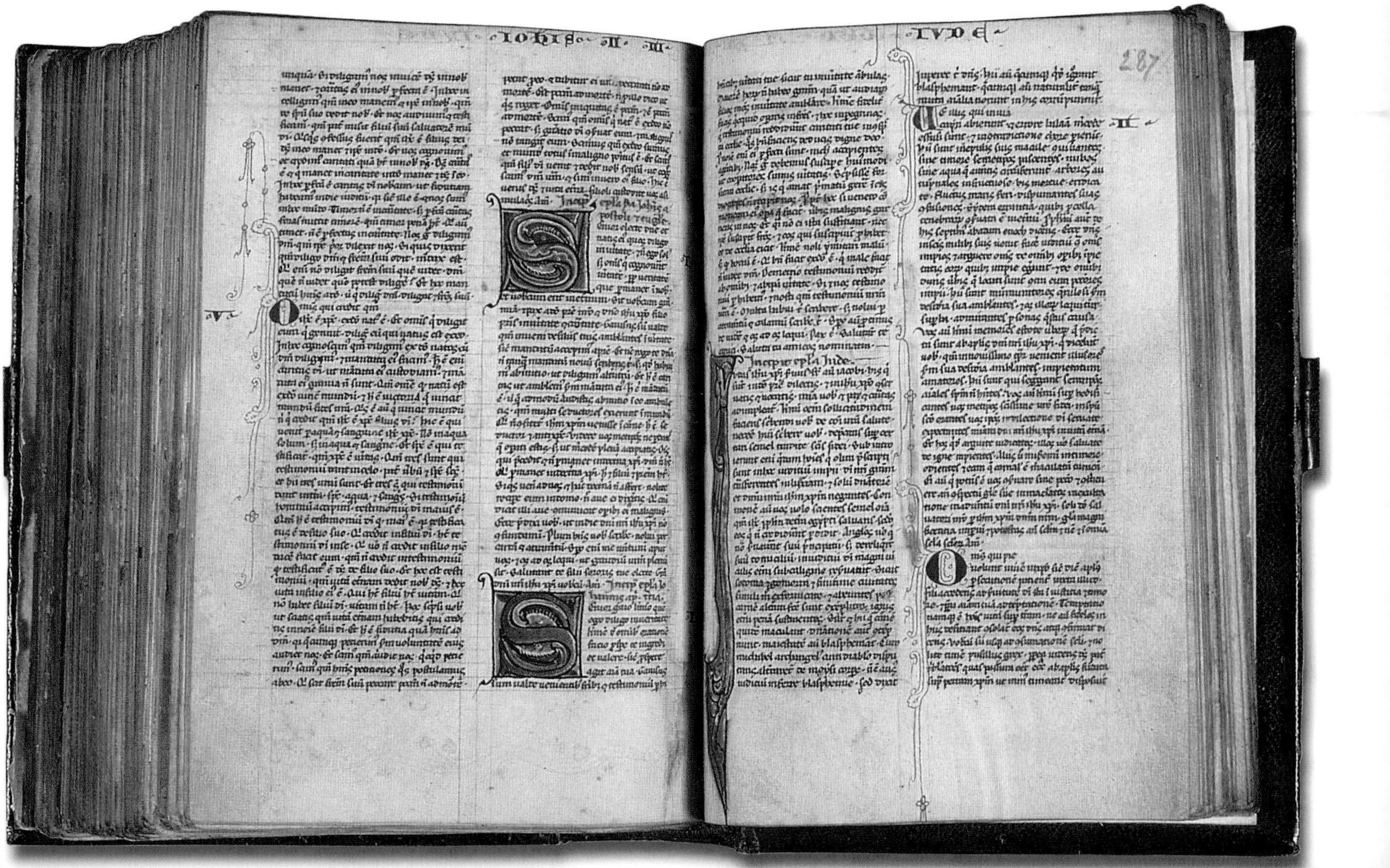
IOHIS II III
IVDE
287

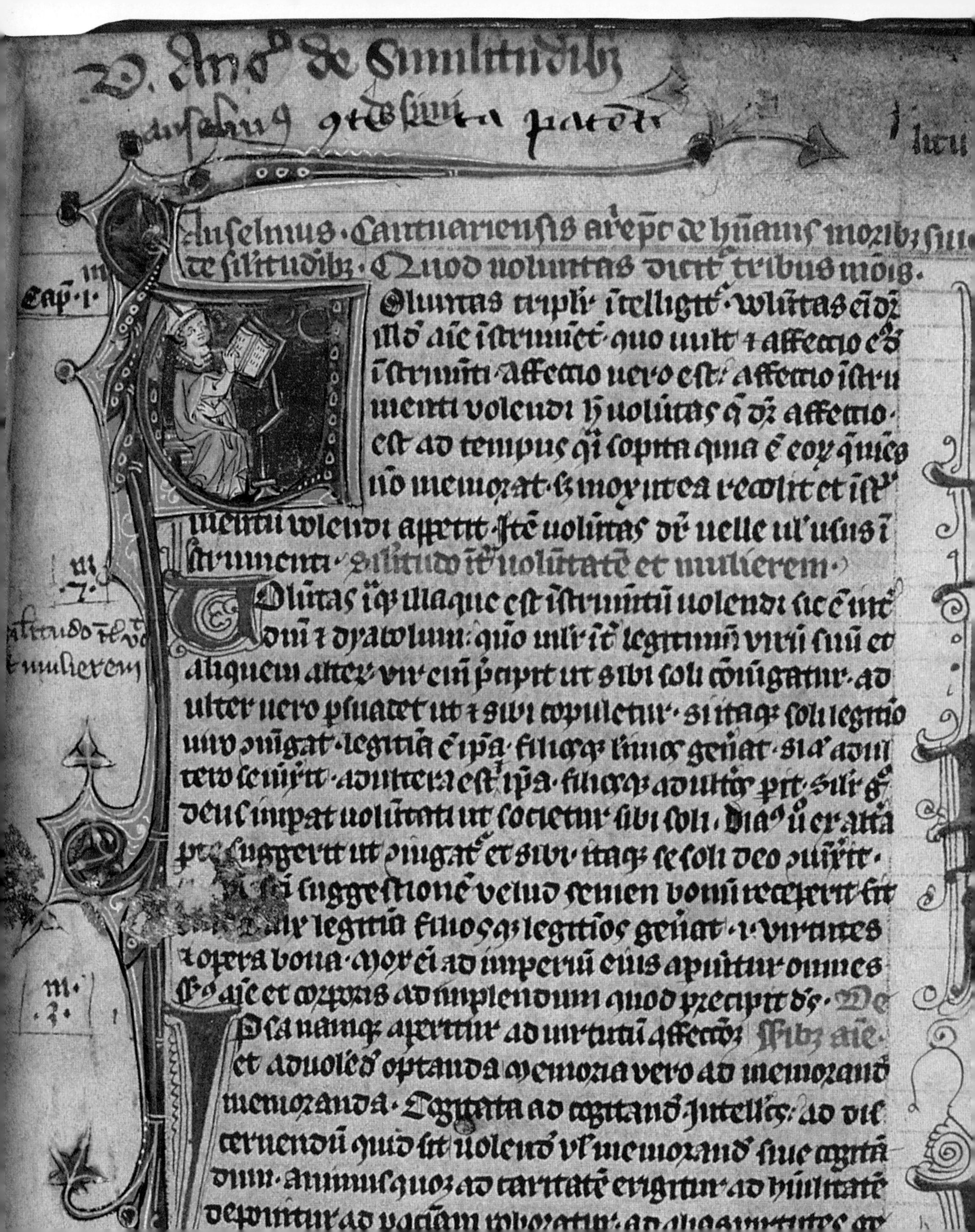

D. Ans° de similitudinibus
Anselmus ... patet

Anselmus · Cantuariensis archiepiscopus de humanis moribus per si-
militudines · Quod voluntas dicitur tribus modis ·

Cap. 1 · Voluntas tripliciter intelligitur · Voluntas enim dicitur
illo anime instrumentum quo vult et affectio est
instrumenti · Affectio vero est affectio instrumenti volendi · Hec voluntas que dicitur affectio
est ad tempus quasi sopita quia est eorum quae
non memorat · sed mox ut ea recolit et instru-
mentum volendi appetit · Item voluntas dicitur velle vel usus instrumenti · Similitudo inter voluntatem et mulierem ·

m. 7 · Similitudo inter voluntatem et mulierem
Voluntas igitur illa que est instrumentum volendi sic est inter
deum et dyabolum quo velut inter legitimum virum suum et
aliquem alterum virum cum precipit ut sibi soli coniugatur · ad-
ulter vero persuadet ut et sibi copuletur · Si itaque soli legitimo
viro coniugatur · legitima est ipsa filiosque legitimos generat · Si autem adul-
tero se iunxerit · adultera est ipsa · filiosque adulterinos parit · Sic et
deus imperat voluntati ut societur sibi soli · Diabolus vero econtra
persuggerit ut coniugatur et sibi · Itaque se soli deo iunxerit ·
... suggestionem velud semen bonum receperit fit
... legitima filiosque legitimos generat · id est virtutes
et opera bona · Mox ei ad imperium eius aperiuntur omnes

m. 3 · sensus anime et corporis ad implendum quod precipit deus · Me-
ipsa namque aperitur ad virtutum affectionem · sensibus anime
et adolescens optanda · Memoria vero ad memorandum
memoranda · Cogitatio ad cogitandum · Intellectus ad dis-
cernendum quid sit volendum vel memorandum sive cogitandum · Animus quoque ad caritatem erigitur · ad humilitatem
deponitur ad vacuam ... ad alias virtutes ...

10

A Durham Monk at University

Anselm, *De similitudinibus; De Concordia.* Augustine, *De libero arbitrio; Sermones de uerbis Domini et Apostoli.*

Parchment manuscript written in England, probably Oxford, in the first third of the 14th century. 142 leaves. 324 x 212 mm (text-block: 250 x 157 mm).

Provenance: Robert Graystanes (d. 1334); Durham Cathedral Priory; George Davenport (1663), by whom given to Cosin's Library, 1670.

Cosin MS V. i. 8

This strikingly-decorated early fourteenth-century manuscript sheds light both on the participation of the northern Benedictines in university education, and on the professional book-trade of medieval Oxford. Though physically one unit, conceptually the volume falls into two parts. The first section (comprising two works by Anselm – *De similitudinibus* and *De Concordia* – plus Augustine's *De libero arbitrio*) holds seminal explorations of free will, mankind's attendant potential for virtue and vice, and the relationship between wilful humanity and an omniscient deity. The remainder contains a popular cycle of Augustine's sermons (*De uerbis Domini et Apostoli*) that formed, in effect, a commentary on the Gospels and Epistles.

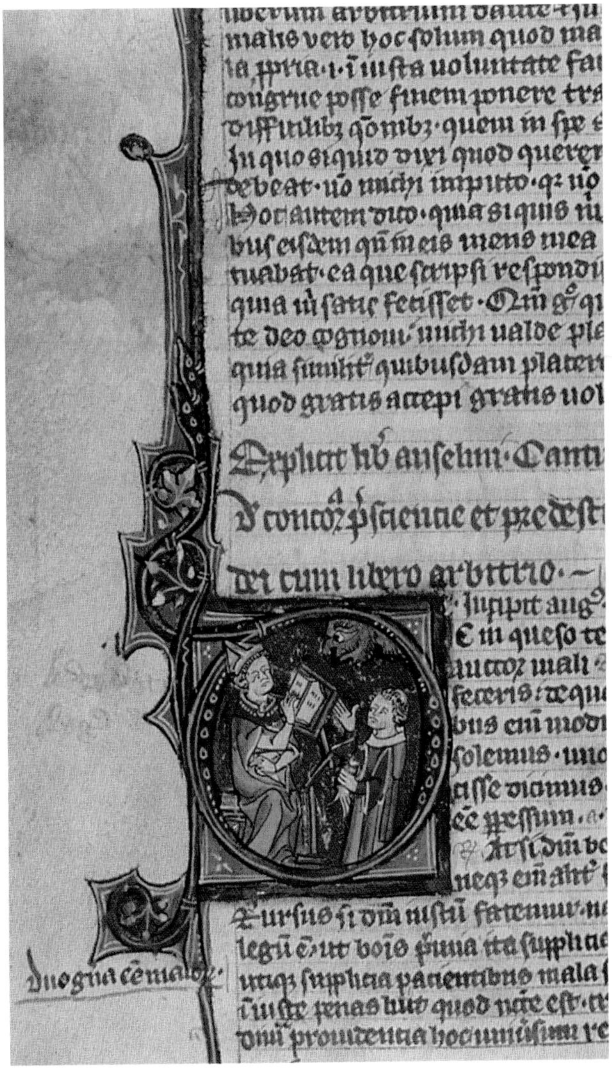

Expeditiously yet clearly written on modest-quality parchment with a standard range of graphic devices to aid the reader, this working book is enhanced by a suite of decorated initials, marking its principal divisions. The six that are historiated feature the author – Anselm or Augustine – in episcopal dress writing at a lectern, generally accompanied by a clerical interlocutor and/or other figures as appropriate. Thus that for *De libero arbitrio* includes a bestial demonic head, doubtless responding to the text's consideration of evil in the world; while those introducing the sermons on the Gospels and Epistles show Augustine at work in the presence of Christ and St Paul respectively. In the lower margins of all but the first of these pages appear pencilled instructions (in Latin) to the illuminator. The first two examples, now difficult to read in full, start: 'A bishop on a throne, writing and in front of him a youth disputing…' and 'A bishop on a throne…'. Then, recoverable in full, we have: 'A bishop on his throne writing and a disciple disputing with him, below God on the one side and a pile of money on the other'; 'A bishop on his throne, writing and speaking with Christ'; and finally, 'A bishop on his throne and St Paul speaking to him, in front of him'. In each case the subject-matter of the historiation conforms to the instructions.

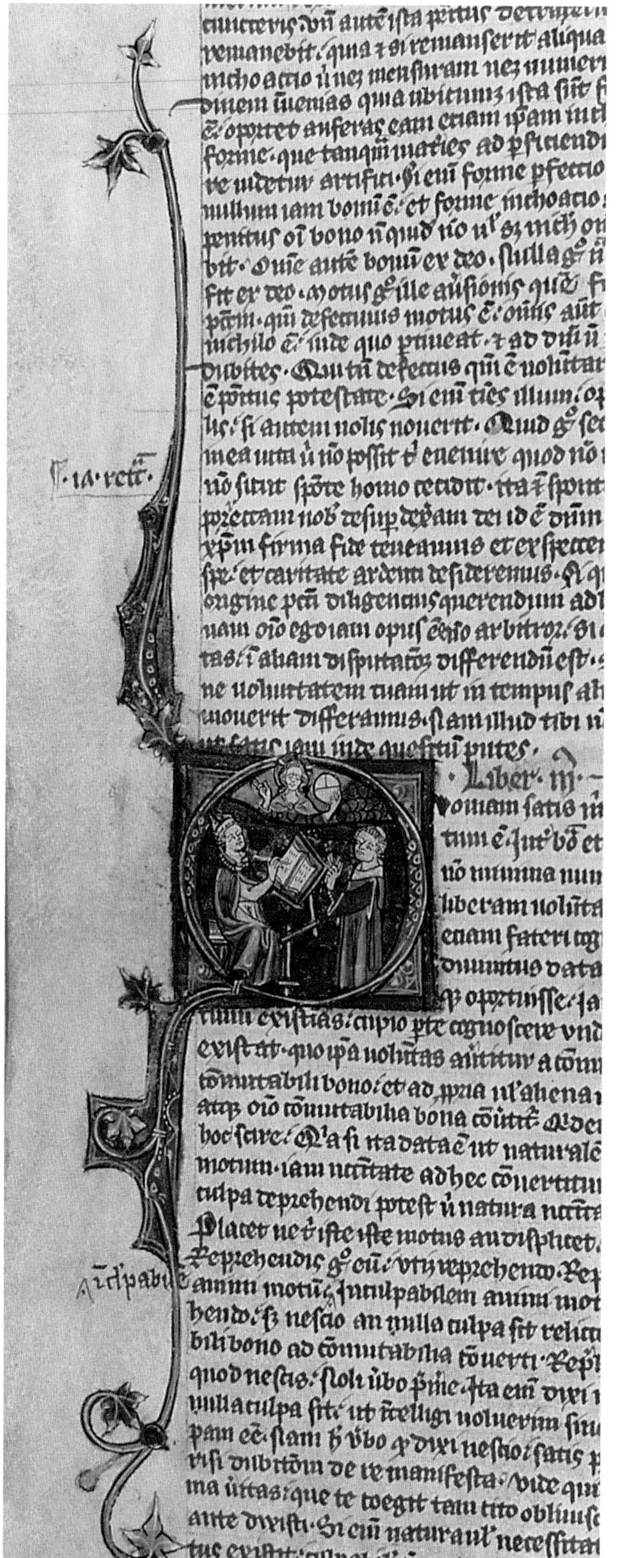

A contemporary inscription at the end of the volume declares: 'The book of St Cuthbert of Durham acquired through Brother Robert of Graystanes'. The monk Robert Graystanes (d. 1334) seems to have spent much of the period from 1306–26 at Oxford, where Durham had recently founded its own study-cell. A Bachelor of Theology by 1315, subsequently a D. Theol., he composed a commentary on the *Sentences* of Peter Lombard, and is uncertainly credited with compiling a chronicle on the church of Durham. Eventually, after a couple of stints as sub-prior of the mother house, he was elected bishop of Durham by the community (1333) – but in the event ceded the post to Richard de Bury (d. 1345), the celebrated bibliophile and author of *Philobiblon*.

During his time at Oxford Graystanes both procured books and pawned them (in the University's loan chests); the present manuscript was doubtless made there. Its texts were duplicates: Durham had an early twelfth-century copy of Augustine's *De uerbis* (Cathedral Library, B. II. 18); while on a list of books sent to the Oxford cell from the mother house in 1315 is a volume of Anselm which includes the works found here. (The tension between providing multiple copies to meet student needs and continuously expanding the range of the collection is one that university libraries still feel today.) Of the six further manuscripts in Durham that preserve Graystanes inscriptions (some just like that in the present book), three have works by or attributed to Augustine, while the others contain Hugh of St Cher's *Concordantia Bibliae*, part of Aquinas' *Summa theologiae*, and Averroes on Aristotle; all remain in the Cathedral Library (A.I.2; B.I.10; B.II.19, 20, and 28; and C.I.18).

Richard Gameson

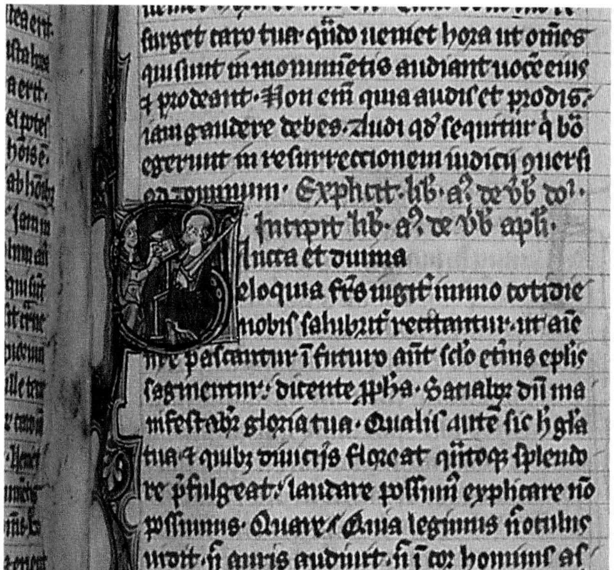

professionem fecit vera confessione ante obitum monachus re-
deleuit. primum dominum ursarium designat, dixit ordinem an-
gelicum. sicut .n. ursarius ursos, ita angeli spiritus malignos
a sua seuicia cohibent et opprimunt ne nobis nocere quantum
nequam volunt. Explicit lib. a. de similitudinibus.
Incipit lib. de concordia prescientie et gratie.

De tribus illis questionibus in quibus dei prescientie atque predestinationi nec
non et gratie liberum arbitrium re
pugnare videtur. quod in deus
dignatur aperire temptabo ipso
adiuvante scribendo ostendere.
Videntur quidem prescientia dei
et liberum arbitrium repugnare. quoniam ea que deus
prescit. necesse est esse futura. et que per liberum ar
bitrium fiunt. nulla necessitate proveniunt. Sed si
repugnant. impossibile est simul et esse prescientiam
dei que omnia previdet et aliquid fieri per liberta
tem arbitrii. Que impossibilitas si abesse intelli
gitur repugnantia que videtur inesse penitus
removetur. Ponamus ergo simul esse et prescientiam dei
quam sequi necessitas futurarum rerum videtur et libertatem
arbitrii per quam multa sine ulla necessitate fieri creduntur
et videamus utrum impossibile sit hec duo simul esse.
Quod si est impossibile. oritur inde aliud impossi
bile. Impossibile siquidem est. quo posito aliud

THOMAS HOCCLEVE'S AUTOGRAPH POEMS FOR JOAN BEAUFORT

11

Thomas Hoccleve, *Complaint, Dialogus cum Amico, etc.*

Parchment manuscript written in England (by the author).
[1] + 2 + 10 + 83 + [1] leaves. 230 x 160 mm.

Provenance: written for Joan Beaufort (d. 1440). Various owners including John Stow, the antiquary (d. 1605) and the poet William Browne of Tavistock (d. 1645?). Acquired in 1664 by George Davenport.

Cosin MS V. iii. 9

Thomas Hoccleve (?1367–1426) spent his working life, from at least 1387, as a clerk in the service of the Privy Seal at Westminster, writing many warrants and other documents for action by other government offices, mostly in French or Latin. He also composed a considerable amount of English verse, in the style and metres of Geoffrey Chaucer who died at Westminster in 1400, and whom he may have known personally. Hoccleve addressed most of his poems to royal, noble or well-placed individuals in the metropolis, and copied selections for some of them, such as the present volume for Joan Countess of Westmorland, done between 1422 and the poet's death in 1426. It contains a lengthy autobiographical dialogue, incorporating an affecting story of a patient empress, in stanzas, with a theological interpretation of it in prose, followed by a verse translation of a dialogue on preparation for death, a prose translation from a church service for All Saints day (with brief remarks on the choice of heaven or hell), and lastly a second story in stanzas, with a dishonest but eventually repentant woman (again with a prose interpretation).

The original first quire is lost and was replaced on paper by the London antiquary John Stow (?1525–1605), copied from a different (unknown) manuscript.

Joan Beaufort (?1379–1440) was one of the children of John of Gaunt, Duke of Lancaster, by his long-time mistress Catherine Swinford, whom he married after the death of his second wife, Constanza of Castile, in 1394. (Chaucer's wife Philippa was Catherine's sister.) Joan's second husband was Ralph Neville, first Earl of Westmorland (d. 1425). She died in 1440 at Howden (E. Yorks.), and was buried with her mother in Lincoln Cathedral, but there is an effigy of her with her husband and his first wife in Staindrop church (Co. Durham), near their Raby Castle. Although the book now in Durham may once have been there or at their nearer Brancepeth Castle, the scribbles on it indicate that in the later sixteenth century it was in West Yorkshire, and Hoccleve's intended presentation had been most probably in the south-east of England.

Hoccleve's hand-writing is an excellent version of the so-called Secretary script which was then used for Privy Seal documents, but here rather larger (as in the two other known autograph selections of his verse), uniform in appearance, except for the more formal dedication at the end – a stanza of envoy to the countess. Hoccleve's signature at the foot of this page has been strengthened with ink at a later date, but under ultra-violet light it can be confirmed as certainly original.

After John Stow, the book belonged to the poet William Browne of Tavistock (*c.* 1590–1645?), who edited its second tale in his *Shepheards Pipe* (1614). In 1664 it was acquired, like four more of Browne's volumes of Middle English poetry, by George Davenport (d. 1677), and was given by him in 1670 with seventy other manuscripts to Bishop Cosin's Library. It was he who wrote 'Perlegi [I have read it through].1666.'

A. I. Doyle

95

Samaritane. I am the welle who so drynkith
of þt watir he shal nat thriste ageyn. After
this Jonathas eet of the fruyt of the second tree
which restored al þt was lost þt is to seyn whan
man is glorified in eternel lyf and helith the kyng
þt is to seyn resoun, and so he entrith the shipp of
the chirche, and to his paines þt is to seyn his flessh
he puruieth watir of contricioun & fruyt of
penance and sharpnesse for which the flessh
þt is to seyn carnel or flesshly affeccion stenteth
and dieth, and the man purchaceth & getith by
penitence the goodes þt weren lost, and so he gooth
in to his contree þt is to seyn the regne of heuene
to which god of his grace brynge vs alle Amen

Ego sum fons q[ui] biberit &c.

Go smal book to the noble excellence
Of my lady of Westmerland and seye
Hir humble seruant with al reuerence
Him recomandith vn to hir noblesse
And byseeche hir on my behalue & preye
Thee to receyue for hir owne right
And looke thow in al manere weye
To plese hir wommanhede do thy might

humble seruant
to your gracious
noblesse
T. Hoccleue

Perlegi 1666

An Illuminated Psalter from Flanders 12

Latin Psalter.

Parchment manuscript written in the Low Countries in the mid-15th century. [2] + 177 + [2] leaves. 176 x 125 mm.

Provenance: inscriptions of members of the Sharp family from the 17th century onwards; armorial bookplate of Thomas Sharp, archdeacon of Northumberland (d. 1758).

Bamburgh Select 25

This attractively decorated fifteenth-century psalter was – like some contemporary Books of Hours – produced in the Low Countries for the English market. Along with the psalms are included the usual canticles, a litany and six collects like those found in York Books of Hours. There are a surprising number of corrections to the Latin, while eventual adaptation to Protestant use is indicated by the addition of Coverdale's Psalm numbering.

Eight of the psalms have colourful historiated initials whose broadly conventional imagery is rich in resonances. The figure of the Fool, most commonly associated with Psalm 52 (53) which describes such a type, here adorns Psalm 51 (52) – a less common usage. Psalm 97 (98) 'Sing a new song unto the Lord' has three singing tonsured figures; while the Trinity illustrates Psalm 109 (110), whose opening verse is used in Acts (e.g. ch. 2) to justify Christ's divinity.

The remaining five all show King David, who was regarded through most of Christian history as the author of the Psalms. Attempts to confirm such authorship by finding corresponding events in the King's life are well illustrated by the historiated initial to Psalm 68 (69). Its opening metaphor ('Save me, O God, for the waters have risen up to my neck') is interpreted literally so that the king is shown lying naked and almost submerged in a river. This Psalm is, after Psalm 22, the most often quoted in relation to Christ (e.g. v.21), and thereby indicates another reason for David's importance – his role not only as the ancestor but also as a prefiguration of Christ. Prophetically, he also anticipates Christ's future significance. Thus in Psalm 26 (27), reflecting on 'the Lord is my light,' he is made to point to his eyes, while in Psalm 38 (39) there is a similar reference to guarding the mouth.

The remaining two allude to David's role as a musician. At Psalm 80 (81), which lists a variety of instruments, he plays on chiming bells, a hammer in each hand. Heading the corpus at Psalm 1, David plays the instrument with which he is most commonly associated, the harp, with God looking on approvingly. If this evokes David's role as composer of the Psalms as a whole, there is a certain irony here, in that, while instruments are frequently mentioned elsewhere in the psalter, none is recorded in Psalm 1. Yet it does speak of blessedness (*Beatus vir*), and such blessedness is commonly associated with music. Indeed, the hanging up of harps is used in Psalm 137 to indicate the depths of the people's despair. Although the Bible speaks of David using the harp to ease Saul's depression, his instrument is more likely to have been a lute, as the harp was a relatively late introduction to Israel. The first Christian images tend to show a lute or psaltery. But the harp became the norm, not least because its stretched sinews could be taken to allude to Christ on the Cross, an image found in Cassiodorus, Bernard of Clairvaux and Lydgate, among others; the Christian altar in our illustration performs the same function.

David Brown

eatus uir q
non abijt in
consilio ipio
rum: et in uia
peccatorū non
stetit: & in ca
thedra pestile
ne non sedit.
ed in lege
dn̄i uolunta
eius: & in lege eius meditabitur die ac nocte
t erit tamq̄ lignū qd plantatum est se
cus decursus aquarum: quod fructū suum
dabit in tempore suo.
t folium eius non defluet: et omnia
quecumq; faciet prosperabuntur.
on sic impii non sic: sed tamq̄ pulvis
quem proicit ventus a facie terre.
deo non resurgūt impii in iudicio: ne
q peccatores in consilio iustorum.
uoniam nouit dominus uiam iustor

plebis sue benedictus deus.
Saluum me fac deus.
quoniam intraue
runt aque usque ad
aiam meam.
Infixus sum
in limo profundi: et non est sub
stancia.
Veni in altitudinem maris: et
tempestas dimersit me.
Laboraui clamans rauce facte

Cantate domino canti
cum nouum: quia
mirabilia fecit.
Saluauit sibi dex
tera eius et brachium
sanctum eius.
Notum fecit dns salutare suum in co
spectu gentium reuelauit iusticiam suam.
Recordatus est misericordie sue: et verita

A Chaucer Manuscript

13

Geoffrey Chaucer, *Troilus and Criseyde*;
Thomas Hoccleve, *Letter of Cupid*; etc.

Parchment manuscript written in England in the mid-15th century.
[1] + 3 + 111 + 2 + [1] leaves. 275 x 175 mm.

Provenance: inscriptions from the 15th and 16th centuries include Robert King and Paul Keyne of London; belonged to the poet William Browne of Tavistock (d. 1645?); acquired in 1664 by George Davenport.

Cosin MS V.ii.13

Geoffrey Chaucer's epic romance, *Troilus and Criseyde*, is one of the greatest medieval English poems. Chaucer (d. 1400) translates and adapts Boccaccio's *Il Filostrato*, drawing on Boethius' *Consolation of Philosophy*, to create a five-book tragedy in 'rime royal' that tells of 'the double sorwe of Troilus', prince of Troy. The story follows the rise and fall of Fortune's wheel, as Troilus is struck by the god of love, to experience extreme love-sickness for the beautiful Criseyde, daughter of the traitor Calchas. Through the subtle machinations of Pandarus, Troilus' friend and Criseyde's uncle, Troilus wins Criseyde's love, but can only look on in anguish as she is sent to the Greek camp in exchange for Antenor. As Troilus waits on the walls of Troy, looking for her return, Criseyde is consoled by the Greek Diomede, and thus becomes the archetypical faithless woman. The work ends as Troilus, killed in battle, looks down from the eighth sphere to laugh at the brittle joys of the world. In telling this celebrated story of betrayal in love, Chaucer addresses profound questions of human existence: the nature of romantic love, the predicament of women in a patriarchal world, the clash between the ideal and the real, and the difficulty of reconciling free will and predetermination.

Of this fine poem (composed in the 1380s), there exist only sixteen full manuscript copies, none earlier than the fifteenth century: the present copy is thus a gem in the Cosin collection. Although not *de luxe*, it is elegant, carefully conceived and in good condition. The poem is written on parchment in an expert 'secretary' hand, and the many flourishes suggest the scribe's pride in his calligraphy – though he omitted or repeated some lines which he and others had to correct. The opening initials of each book are in blue decorated with red infilling and flourishing; *incipits* and *explicits* are enlarged and underlined, and touched in red; paraphs to stanzas are marked in red or blue; side notes are also underlined.

Following *Troilus and Criseyde* and written in a less expert hand is Thomas Hoccleve's *Letter of Cupid*, based on a French poem by Christine de Pisan (d. 1425). A careful attempt has been made to imitate the first scribe's presentation. The Letter is followed by the only known copy of a courtly love poem of five seven-line stanzas, 'Not long agoo purposyd I and thought'. The choice of texts, and the side notes highlighting Troilus' lyric songs, imply that the manuscript was expanded as a collection of verse on courtly love. The addition in a later hand of two versions of a short courtly love poem at the front, and two lines from this at the end, 'Whan euery woo hath ease: . . . Be easyd of hys smart', suggests that the manuscript continued to be read in this manner – as a book narrating the experiences and poetry of love, which might offer some ease to the lover's pains.

Corinne Saunders

W Browne.

Chaucer's fibe books of Troilus & Chreseide.

The double sorow of troilus to telle
þat was the king Priamus sonne of Troye
In louyng how þat his auentures felle
ffrom wo to wel and after out of Ioye
My purpos is or þat I parte fro you
Te Tesiphone you helpe me to endite
þis woful vers þat wepen as I write
To the clepe I goddes of torment
þow cruelle fury sorowyng euer in peyn
helpe me þat am þe sorowfull instrument
That helpeth louers as I can to pleyn
ffor wele sitt it the soth to sayn
A woful wight to haue a drery fere
And to a sorowfull tale a sory chere
ffor I þat god of loues suant sue
Ne dar to loue for myn unliklynes
Prayen for spede al should I therfore sterue
So ferre I am from his helpe in derknes
But natheles of þis may don gladnes
Vnto any louer and his cause auaile
haue he my thonke and myne be þis trauaile
But ye louers þat bathen in gladnesse
If any drope of pite in you bee
Remembreth you on passed heuynesse
þat ye haue felt and on þe aduersite
Of oþer folk and thenketh how þat ye
haue felt þat loue durst you displeas
Or ye haue wonne him with to great an ease
And prayeth for hem þat ben in þe case
Of troylus as ye may after here
That loue him bring in heuen to solace
And eke for me prayeth to god so dere
That I haue might to shew on som manere
Such peyn and wo as loues folk endure

× Thesiphone.

it was eid to litill / And so whan he sholde die he
myght not receyue the sacrament for dreed of castinge.
And so he wisshe his side in the clenist wise and heled
it with with a clene clothe of sendil. and so leid there
þe sacrament and seid thus / Lord god þou knowist well
that I loue þe & wolde right feyne receyue the
and I durst with my mouth / ¶ But bicause þat
I may not / I leie the on that plase þat is next myn
herte ÷ and so I shew þe myn herte and my loue /
And so forthwith in sight of all men his side opyned.
and þe ost went into þe side ÷ and so closid ayene
and anone after he yaue up þe spirit / ¶ Thus must
ye loue the sacrament of goddis bodie in your life.
and than he wolle succour youe in your deeth /
¶ The fourth. cause whi þe sacrament is vsed
on the Aulter ÷ is for grete mede geting to euery
man & woman that parfitlie bileuith þerin ffor though
it hath þe liknesse of bred & tast also ÷ yit he must
parfitly beleue that it is verrie goddis bodie the which
he toke in þe virgyn and after died on þe crosse &
rose from deeth to life. and now sittith on his
fadirs right honde ÷ and shal com to deme þe quik
and þe deed / Than he þat thus receyuith it in his
bileue ÷ he getith to him the kingdome of heuen
And he that louith not þe sacrament and receyuith
it ÷ he receyuith his owne dampnacion into the
payne that eid shal last / Than for to sharp your
bileue ÷ I tell youe this ensample ¶ I rede how
ther was in the tyme of Seynt Grigorie a woman
that hight Lasyna. which made vnto þe pope
singing brede / And so on a tyme whan he howsilld
the people. he cam to this woman & saide ÷ take here

gode body passid a very
short way into this mans
hart.

Preaching and Response in the Fifteenth and Sixteenth Centuries

14

John Mirk, *Festial.*

Paper and parchment manuscript written in England (?Leicestershire) in the mid-15th century. [1] + 1 + 165 + 1 + 2 + [1] leaves. 260 x 197 mm.

Provenance: possibly used for a printed edition in Paris or the Low Countries; inscriptions of members of the North family of London and Canterbury; acquired by John Cosin before the Civil War and amongst the books he left in Peterhouse, Cambridge *c.* 1644, which he removed to Durham in the late 1660s.

Cosin MS V.iii.5

The *Festial*, a collection of sermons in English, was drawn up in the late fourteenth century by John Mirk, an Augustinian canon of Lilleshall Abbey, Shropshire. The version in the present manuscript consists of sixty-one sermons with a prefatory prayer and prologue. The text was expertly written by a single hand in a set 'secretary' script with occasional calligraphic flourishes; it is articulated with blue and red initials, paraphs and sentence capitals; Latin phrases and English names are in red. The image of a cleric standing in a hexagonal pulpit that adorns the first initial advertises the purpose of the work.

First printed by Caxton in 1483, Mirk's *Festial* became probably the most frequently printed work in English prior to the Reformation. Its popularity in the fifteenth century, evidenced by the existence of at least thirty manuscripts, was no doubt due in part to its direct and colloquial tone and its relative simplicity of thought, but also to the fact that it provided sermons of an orthodox nature at a time when Lollard preaching had been suppressed. The orthodoxy of its sentiments, however, caused it to be attacked in the Reformation. In this manuscript, for example, the word 'pope' has frequently been erased, and some references to purgatory and to Thomas Becket were also deleted. Our book was extensively annotated in English in the sixteenth century, with underlining or bracketing of the relevant text. These markings are particularly dense in the sermon for Corpus Christi, part of which (f. 50v) is reproduced here. Near the foot of the page the word 'pope' has been erased, then reinstated. The underlined passage recounts the tale of a man who could not swallow the sacrament 'for dreed of casting' (vomiting), and so had it laid on his breast, whereupon it was miraculously subsumed. The annotation notes that God's body 'passed a very short way' into the man's heart: whether this is credulous or derisory is not clear, but at some other points in the sermon the annotator presumably approved of Mirk's sentiment, as where he underlined a passage (f. 50r) which declares that if birds are mindful of Christ's passion 'moche more sholde man haue remembraunce whiche was bought with his preciouse blood'. In any case, the annotations and erasures testify to the fact that people continued to engage with this manuscript and its contents in the sixteenth century.

David Ashurst

Graunt vs alle goode endyng. And in heuen to haue
a wonnyng. Amen. Amen for charite.
Explicit vita sancti Alberi confessoris.

Here begynneth the prolog of the holy seynt
seynt Margarete. compendyously compiled
in balade by lidgate dan John monk of Bury. Ao viii h. vi.

As the Reuerence of seynt Margarete.
My purpos is hir lyfe to compile.
Though I haue no Rethorikes swete.
Nor colours noon tenbelisshe with my style.
yet dar I seyn it happeth so somen while.
Vnder writyng rude of apparence.
Mater is hid of grete intellygence.

Ful ofte falleth in these Chestys blake.
Golde and perlys and stones of grete prys.
Ben ylooke and in to warde ytake.
And by sentence and the prudent avys.
Of philosoffres that holden were so wys.
A. royal Ruby in whiche ther is no lak.
May closed ben in a ful pore sak.

And though that I haue noon eloquence.
For to discryue hir parfit holynesse.
Her chaste lyf hir tendre Innocence.
Hir martirdam wrought by grete duresse
Ay vnmutable in hir stablenesse.
Vn to the dethe ay one in hir suffraunce.
So was hir herte roted on constaunce.

In crystes feith she gan hir so delyte.
For whom she lyste despyse al worldly glorye.
This daysye with leves rede and white.
Purpul hewed as maked is memorye.
Whan that hir blode was shad oute by victorye.

Marriage and Chastity in Middle English

15

John Lydgate, *Siege of Thebes.* The Life of St Alexis. Lydgate, *Life of St Margaret.* Etc.

Parchment manuscript written in England in the mid-15th century.
[1] + 3 + 111 + 2 + [1] leaves. 295 x 185 mm.

Provenance: various early and mid-16th-century ownership inscriptions including James Elwood of Canterbury and Thomas Peyton; belonged to the poet, William Browne of Tavistock (d. 1645?); acquired in 1664 by George Davenport.

Cosin MS V.ii.14

The rubric on fol. 97v of this mid-fifteenth-century manuscript marks the end of one tale of saintly chastity heroically defended ('Explicit vita sancti Alexi confessoris...') and the beginning of another ('Here begynneth the prolog of the holy seynt seynt Margarete...'). The story of St Alexis begins with the marriage of its aristocratic protagonist to 'a mayden good and of gret honour' and his decision, on their wedding-night, to abandon her in favour of a life of anonymous poverty. Before he departs, however, he instructs her on the importance of virginity ('he preched hir with al his myght/ of synne that she shulde haue no plyght,/ but holde hir maydenhede'). At the same time, as if to emphasize the continuing validity of their marital bond despite their physical separation, he gives her a golden ring which she is to keep in memory of him. She remains in the household, but it is only thirty-four years later that she rediscovers Alexis, and then only after his death. It transpires that for half that time he has been living there as a dependent pauper – unrecognized because of the hardships that he has undergone. The pathos of this dénouement is exploited to the full, with the bride movingly lamenting both her own widowhood and the loss of the man she describes as her 'hope of joye' and the 'myrour... that my lykeng was ynne'.

St Margaret's defence of her chastity is just as heroic. Like Alexis, she faces the temptation of an honourable marriage, in this case to the prefect of Antioch who promises to 'loue and cherysshe' her 'duryng al my lyfe,/ that atwene vs ther shal be no strife'; but when she rejects his offer, her suitor has her tortured and thrown into gaol. There she encounters a 'felle dragoun' who attempts to swallow her, but – apparently finding her holiness indigestible – bursts asunder. After various other torments the saint is eventually 'released' by decapitation; and the legend concludes by emphasizing her power to intercede for women in childbirth.

The author of this version of the legend of St Alexis (which survives in three other manuscripts) remains anonymous; but that of St Margaret (which survives in eight) is ascribed here and elsewhere to one of Chaucer's most prolific followers. It was, we are told, 'compendyously compiled in balade by lidgate, Dan Johan Monk of Bury' – that is 'succinctly' and 'in stanzas' by Master John Lydgate (*c.* 1370–1449/50?), monk of the wealthy Benedictine abbey of Bury St Edmunds. Succinctness is not the quality that springs most readily to mind in connection with Lydgate; and indeed Cosin V. ii. 14 also contains a more extended work by the monk, *The Siege of Thebes* – a readable, but characteristically diffuse, romance of some 5,000 lines, treating the saga of Oedipus, his sons, and the Argive expedition against Thebes. Another text in the manuscript (a verse translation of the *Distichs* of Cato) was written by one of Lydgate's avowed followers, Benedict Burgh (d. by 1483). Its remaining item is another hagiographical work, a prose life of Mary Magdalene.

Neil Cartlidge

An Early Edition of Augustine's *City of God*

16

Augustine of Hippo, *De civitate Dei.*

Strasbourg: Johann Menthelin, in or before 1468.

[334] leaves. 2°. 400 x 300 mm. Binding: 15th-century undecorated wooden boards, traces of clasps and holes for a chain on back board, manuscript title label on front board; rebacked in the 19th century.

Provenance: armorial bookplate and stamp of Continental religious houses; Martin Routh (Routh 3.A.9).

SR.3.B.1

The oldest printed book in the university's collection is the present copy of *City of God* by Augustine of Hippo (354–430). Begun around 412 and written over the course of ten to fifteen years, this encyclopaedic work describes the course of the city of God from the fall of the angels, through creation, sacred and secular history, to its final end in heaven. The city of God is not, as many medieval theologians tended to conclude, synonymous with the Church or any other earthly institution, but is, as it were, the communion of saints – the earthly and heavenly fellowship of those elected by God's grace from the mass of sinful humanity, to believe in, hope for, and love him. The work traces the history of the city of God in contradistinction to the earthly city. To the latter belong all those who have not been elected by God, who remain subject to the consequences of the Fall, who turn away from God by proudly failing to recognise their created dependence upon him, and who put themselves before God, pursuing their own interests or, motivated by a lust for dominion, seek to rule others. The history of these two cities is illustrated both in relation to sacred scriptural history, and also in relation to secular world history: it is demonstrated in Cain and Abel as well as Romulus and Remus; in the history of Israel and the Church as well as that of the Roman Empire. God's just judgement and gracious mercy are demonstrated in both. It is often said that the work was written in response to the fall of Rome in 410, a crisis pagans blamed on the Christians' neglect of the gods who protected the Empire, while Christians were faced with the question of God's providence in relation to what they had increasingly come to regard as a Christian Empire. However, it is clear that Augustine's theology of the Fall of Man was already leading him to expound these ideas in relation to Christian life in the world as one of eschatological longing for the peace and justice of the heavenly kingdom which can never be attained in this life, and that he would have articulated them whether Rome had fallen or not.

The *City of God* was tremendously popular throughout the Middle Ages and was perhaps more widely copied and read than any of Augustine's other works (with the exception of the *Confessions*). There are literally hundreds of manuscripts, dating from the fifth century onwards; and by the end of the fifteenth century more than twenty printed editions had been produced. Though not the *editio princeps* (that was done at Subiaco in 1467), our copy is the first edition to include a commentary. Books 1–10.29 are covered by the Dominican, Thomas Waleys (d. 1350), the remainder (10.29–22.30) being taken from the terser exposition of his fellow Dominican, Nicholas Trevet (d. *c.* 1334). The grand format, layout, typefaces and hand-inserted rubrication all imitate the conventions of contemporary institutional manuscript copies, underlining the extent to which printing was indebted to earlier traditions of book-making.

Carol Harrison

Incipit liber octauꝰ de ciuitate dei beati Augustini

Nunc itētiōe nobꝭ opꝰ ē aīo mlˡto q̄ȝ erat : ī supiorꝝ solucōe q̄ōnū et explicacōe librorꝝ . De theologia quippe quā natˀalē vocāt . nō cū q̄buslibȝ hoībꝫ . nō enī fabulosa ē vlˡ ciuilis hoc est ulˡ vrbana vlˡ theatˀca . quarꝝ altera lactitat deorū cˀmīa/altera indicat deorꝝ desideria cˀmīosiora/ac ꝑ hoc malignorꝝ pociꝰ demoniū q̄ȝ deorꝝ . ſȝ cū philosophis ē habēda colacio : q̊rꝝ ipm nomē si latine intˀpretem̄ amorē sapīe ꝓfitetˀ. Porro si sapīa deꝰ ē/ꝑ quē facta sūt oīa . sicut diuīa auc̄tas veritasq̄ȝ mōstrauit : verꝰ phs est amator dei . ſȝ q̇a res ipa cꝰ hoc nomē ē nō ē ī oībꝰ q̇ hoc nomīe gloiantˀ . neq̄ȝ enī ꝯtinuo vere sapīe sūt amatores/q̇cūq̄ȝ appellantˀ philosophi : ꝓfecto ex oībꝫ q̊rꝝ sentēcias litteris nosse potuimꝰ eligēdi sūt . cū q̇bus non indigne q̄stio ista tractetˀ .

Quod supsticiōes sūt abiciēde et v̇e rˀligiones colēde . de phīa et q̄ verꝰ phs ē amator & cultor veri dei .

Neq̄ȝ enī hoc opē oēs omniū phorꝝ vanas opīōes rˀfutare suscepi . ſȝ eas tm̄ q̄ ad theologiā ꝑtinēt . q̄ v̇bo grˀero significari ītelligimꝰ de diuīitate rōne siue ſmonē . nec eas oīm ſȝ eorꝝ tātū . q̇ cū et esse diuīitatē et hūana curare ꝯsenciāt . nō tamē sufficere vniꝰ īcōmutabilis dei cultū ad uitā adipiscēdā eciā post mortē beatā . Sȝ mlˡtos ab illo sane vno ꝯditos atq̄ȝ institutos ob eā causā colēdos putāt Hij iā eciā varronis opinionē : veritatis ꝓpinq̇tate trāscēdūt . Siq̇dē ille totā theologiā natˀalē vsq̄ȝ ad m̄dm istū visibilē vlˡ aīmā eiꝰ extēdere potuit . isti vero supˀ oēȝ aīe natˀam ꝯfitentˀ deū . q̇ nō solū mūdū visibilē q̇ sepe celi & tˀre nomīe nūcupatˀ. Sed eciā omēȝ omnīo aīaȝ fe

De opīōe varroīs de theologia natˀali de mūdo visibili vlˡ aīa et de theologia ītellectuali .

cerit/et q̇ rōnalē et ītellectualē cuiꝰ generis aīa hūana ē/participacōe sui luminis incōmutabilis/et īcorporei beatā facit . Hos phos platōicos appellatos a platōe doctore vocabulo diriuato nullꝰ q̇ hec vlˡ tenuerit audiuit ignoratˀ. Cap ij

Ne hoc igitˀ platōe q̄ necessaria pūti q̄stioni existimo breuitˀ attigā ꝑus illos ꝯmemorās q̇ eū ī eodē generè lrārꝝ tēpore p̄cesserūt . Quātū enim attiet ad lrās grˀcas/q̄ ligua īt ceteras genciū clarior habetur duo phorꝝ genera tradūtur : vnū ytalicū ex ea ꝑte ytalie q̄ quōdā magna grˀcia nūcupata ē . Alterꝝ ionicū ī eis tˀris/vbi & nūc grˀcia noīata est . ytalicū genꝰ auctorē habuit pithagorā samiū : a q̊ eciā ferūt ipm philosophie nomē exortū . Nā cū āna sapiētes appellarentur . q̇ mō quodā alijs p̄stare videbantˀ. Iste ītrogatꝰ q̇d ꝓfiteretˀ/phm se rˀspōdit/id ē studiosū vlˡ amatorē sapīe : q̄ñ sapiētē ꝓfiteri arrogātissimū videbatur . Ionica v̇o gn̄is princeps fuit thales milesiꝰ vnꝰ illorꝝ septē q̇ sūt appellati sapiētes . ſȝ illi sex vite generè distīguebātur : ex q̇busdā p̄ceptis ad bene viuēdū accōmodatis . Iste aūt thales ut successores eciā ꝓpagaret/rerꝝ naturā scrutatus . suasq̄ȝ disputacōes littˀis mādās/enituit maximeq̄ȝ admirabilis extitit : q̄ astrologie numeris ꝯphēsis . defcꝰ solis et lune eciā p̄dicē potuit . Aquā tamē putauit rerū eē p̄ncipiū . Hinc oīa elemēta mūdi ipm q̄ȝ mūdū & q̄ ī eo ꝑgignūtˀ existē . Nichil aūt huic operi . q̄ mūdo cōsiderato tā mirabile asspicimꝰ : ex diuīa mēte ꝓposuit . Huic sucessit anaximāder eiꝰ auditō : mutauitq̄ȝ de rerꝝ natˀa opinioēȝ . Non enī ex vna re sicˀ thales ex humore/sed ex suis proprijs

Duo gn̄a phorum vnū ytalicū alterꝝ ionicum .

Thales millesimꝰ princeps ionica generis aquā eē putauit rerꝝ principium .

Anaximāder ex ꝓprijs prīcipijs q̄sq̄ȝ res nasci putauit .

lactitat

laudabilius

beati

An Early Edition of Virgil

17

Virgil, *Buccolica et Georgica; Aeneis.* Juvenal and Persius, *Satyrae.*

Louvain: printed by Johannes de Westfalia, 1475–76.

66; 96; 87 leaves. 2°. 290 x 215 mm.

Provenance: owned by Thomas Cranston, canon of St Andrews who became abbot of Jedburgh in 1484.

Bamburgh Select 7

Early printed texts were generally marketed either just as sheets or in flimsy wrappers; binding them would represent an extra expense for the customer. Thus for economy as much as convenience, a purchaser of several items of the same format might opt to have them bound together as a *Sammelband* (collection-volume). Exemplifying the phenomenon, the present item contains three discrete publications from the press of Johannes de Westfalia – Virgil's *Georgics* and *Eclogues* (printed in 1475), and *Aeneid* (1476), as well as the *Satires* of Juvenal and Persius (1475) – within one, well-preserved, contemporary Flemish binding.

Johannes of Paderborn/Westfalia was one of the founders of printing in the Low Countries, pioneering the use of Roman type there; he described his method of producing books (i.e. printing) as: 'by a certain most modern technique of making letters'. In 1473, as William Caxton was starting his operation at Bruges, Johannes, along with Thierry Martens (cf. no. 25), began at Alost. The following year Johannes moved to the University of Louvain, which furnished a ready home market for his output. He was also energetic in cultivating a wider clientele: customs rolls reveal that from 1478–91 he was marketing his books in England, and in 1483 he paid a personal visit to the stationer of Oxford University. Correspondingly, the role of Louvain in supplying books to England and Scotland peaked in the 1480s when it accounted for 9% and 17% of their literary imports respectively. The present *Sammelband* of Johannes's editions was, as a hand-written inscription and content-list demonstrate, soon in the possession of Thomas Cranston, canon of Saint Andrews – presumably before 1484 when he became abbot of Jedburgh.

The *editio princeps* of Virgil's oeuvre was published in Rome in 1469; Johannes' *Aeneid* was the first publication of that work alone. By 1500 the number of editions of some or all of the poet's corpus stood at around 170. This graphic testimony to Virgil's status and popularity was matched by a continuing freedom of approach to his canon.

In addition to the three main works of Virgil (d. 19 BC), whom Johannes hails as the *princeps poetarum* ('the first among poets'), this part of the volume contains other poems which are the result of imaginative forgery. Thus both the Georgics and the *Aeneid* are prefaced by a synopsis which is ascribed to Publius Ovidius Naso (d. 17 AD) – a claim that will amuse anyone who has read an authentic line of Ovid's work. The plot summary of the Aeneid, for instance, concludes with *ultimus imponit bello turni nece finem* ('The last book brings the war to an end with the death of Turnus'), a banal statement of fact utterly unworthy of Ovidian ésprit. Likewise, after the *Georgics*, the edition contains some tractatuli which earlier ages regarded as youthful works of Virgil that predate the *Eclogues*. Examples include the *carmen de copa* (on a woman running a tavern), a poem on the life of the rose as an allegory for the frailty of human existence, or a poem about the import of the monosyllables *est* and *non* in human speech. They fall rather short of the 'divine song' (*divinum carmen*) that the 'inspired poet' (*vates*) produced in the *Georgics* (the quotations come from the summary that precedes Book III). These charming trifles reflect an age when authorship was a rather more fluid concept than it is today, with authenticity, copyright and royalties hardly contentious issues – though with the advent of printing this was starting to change. Thus poetasters hid behind the names of their famous forbears and their products were in turn employed to flesh out the biographies and the oeuvres of great classical authors. Whether many Renaissance or early modern readers will have reached the Virgilian apocrypha is, however, another matter: the interlinear and marginal comments of the studious reader who annotated the book peter out midway through the eighth *Eclogue*.

Ingo Gildenhard and Richard Gameson

Publii Virgilii Maronis bucolicorum prima egloga incipit feliciter. Melibeus Titirus

Titire tu patule recubans sub tegmine fagi/
Siluestrem tenui musam meditaris auena.
Nos patrie fines/ et dulcia linquimus arua.
Nos patriam fugimus. tu titire lentus in umbra/
Formosam resonare doces amarillida siluas;
O melibee/ deus nobis hec ocia fecit:
Nanque erit ille mihi semper deus. illius aram
Sepe tener nostris ab ouilibus imbuet agnus.
Ille meas errare boues vt cernis/ et ipsam
Ludere que vellem calamo permisit agresti;
Non equidem inuideo: miror magis vndique totis
Usque adeo turbatur agris. en ipse capellas
Protenus eger ago/ hanc etiam vix titire duco
Hic inter densas corilos. modo nanque gemellos
Spem gregis/ ha silice in nuda conixa reliquit.
Sepe malum hoc nobis (si mens non leua fuisset)
De celo tactas memini predicere quercus. Sepe malum hoc nobis si mens non leua fuisset
Sed tamen iste deus quis sit da titire nobis;
Urbem quam dicunt rhomam/ melibee/ putaui
Stultus ego huic nostre similem. quo sepe solemus
Pastores ouium teneros depellere fetus.

Argumētū ouidii naſonis in libros eneidū

Primꝰ habet/ libicā veniāt vt troes i
Edocet excidium troie/ clademq; ſe
Tertius a troia vectos canit equor
Quartus item miſere duo vulnera narrat
Manibus ad tumulum quinto celebrantur
Eneam memorat viſentem tartara ſextus;
In phriges italiam bello iam ſeptimus arm
Dat ſimul enee ſocios octauus ⁊ arma;
Daunius expugnat nono noua menia troie
Exponit decimus tuſcorum in litore pugnas
Undecimo rutuli ſuperant̄ morte camille;
Ultimus imponit bello turni nece finem;

Argumentum primi libri eneidum;

Eneas primo libie depellitur oris
Uir magnus bello/ nulli pietate ſec
Eneas odiis preſſus iunonis iniqu
Italiam querens ſiculis errauit in vndis.
Iactatus tandem libie peruenit ad oras.
Ignaruſq; loci/ fido comitatus achate:
Indicio matris/ regnum cognouit eliſſe.
Quinetiam nebula ſeptus/ peruenit ad vrbe
Arreptoſq; vndis ſocios cum claſſe recepit.
Hoſpitioq; vſus didonis per cuncta benign
Excidium troie iuſſus narrare parabat;

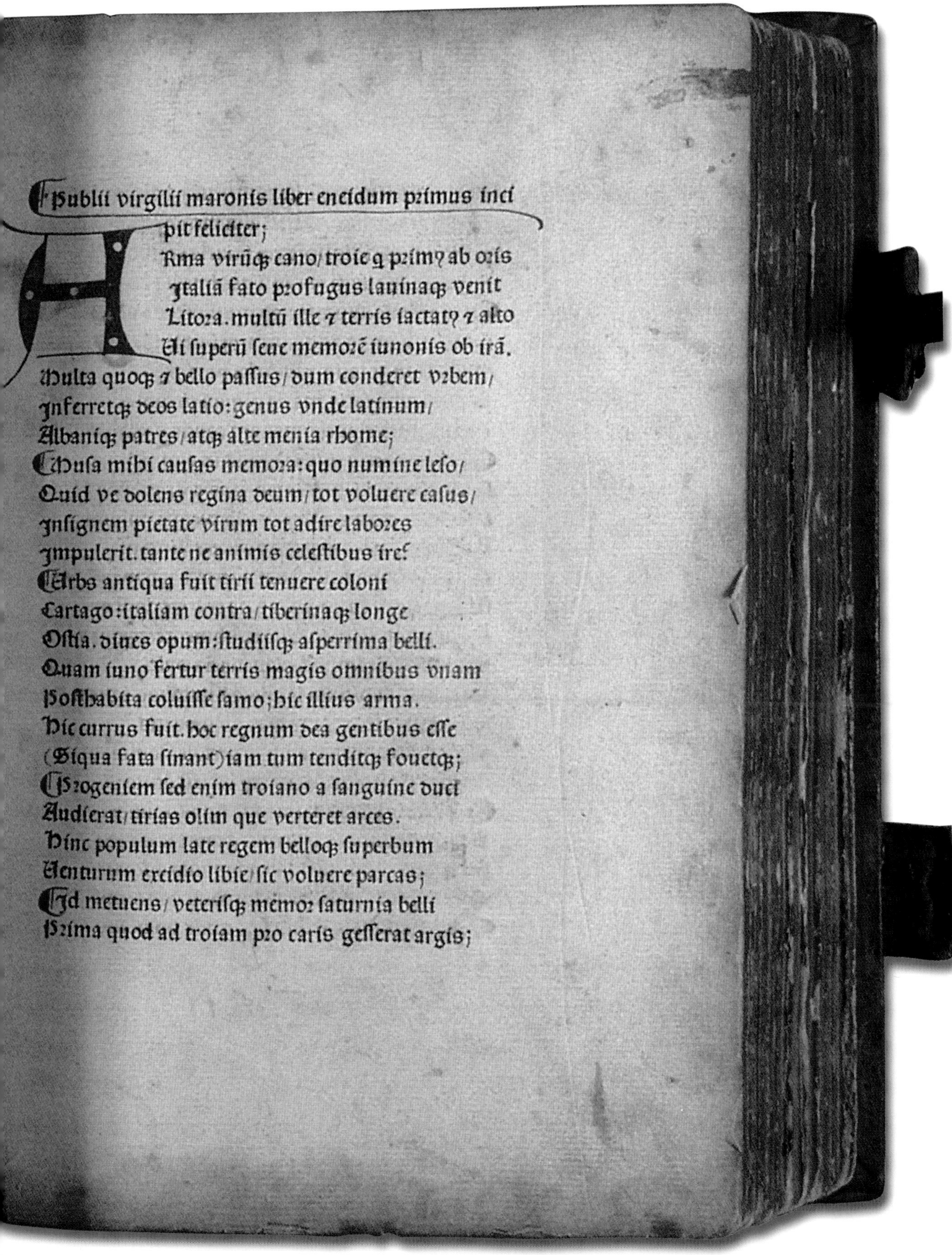

Publii virgilii maronis liber eneidum primus incipit feliciter;

Arma virūq; cano/ troie q prim⁹ ab oris
Italiā fato profugus lauinaq; venit
Litora. multū ille ⁊ terris iactat⁹ ⁊ alto
Ui superū seue memorē iunonis ob irā.
Multa quoq; ⁊ bello passus/ dum conderet vrbem/
Inferretq; deos latio: genus vnde latinum/
Albaniq; patres/ atq; alte menia rhome;
Musa mihi causas memora: quo numine leso/
Quid ve dolens regina deum/ tot voluere casus/
Insignem pietate virum tot adire labores
Impulerit. tante ne animis celestibus ire?
Urbs antiqua fuit tirii tenuere coloni
Cartago: italiam contra/ tiberinaq; longe
Ostia. diues opum: studiisq; asperrima belli.
Quam iuno fertur terris magis omnibus vnam
Posthabita coluisse samo; hic illius arma.
Hic currus fuit. hoc regnum dea gentibus esse
(Siqua fata sinant) iam tum tenditq; fouetq;
Progeniem sed enim troiano a sanguine duci
Audierat/ tirias olim que verteret arces.
Hinc populum late regem belloq; superbum
Uenturum excidio libie/ sic voluere parcas;
Id metuens/ veterisq; memor saturnia belli
Prima quod ad troiam pro caris gesserat argis;

Frensshe	Englissh
Lieuin le brasseur.	Lyeuyn the brewar
Brasse tant de ceruoyse.	Breweth so moche ale.
Quil ne peult vendre	That he may not selle it.
Car il est renommees	For he is renomed.
De mauuais beuurage	Of euyll drynke.
Se luy conuient a le fois.	So hym behoueth other whyle
Jetter deuant les porciaux	To cast to fore the hogges.
Lamfroy le couureur de tieulles.	Lamfroy the couerar of tyles
Couury le belfroy	Couerd the steple.
Descailles de tieulles	With skaylles with tyles.
Au mieulx quil pouoit.	The beste wyse that he may.
Encordont esty.	Neuertheles is it
Par le vent descouuert	By the wynde discouerid
Leonard le couureur destrain	Lenard the thacher
Couury ma maysoncelle	Hath couerd my litell hous.
Destrain et de gluy	With straw and with reed
Les lattes quil achatta.	The lattes that he bought.
Ne valent riens	Be nothyng worth
Il fist les parois.	He made the wallis
Et les placqua de terre.	And daubed them with erthe
Dont est il placqueur	Wherof he was dawber
Logier le feultier.	Logier the feltmaker
A maint bon chappeau	Hath many a good hatte
De beuures et de feultre.	Of beuer and of felte.
Lucien le gantiers	Lucian the glouer
Siet decoste moy.	Sitteth beside me
Faitte gans de cerf	Maketh glouues of an herte
De chien et de brebis.	Of hound and of sheep
Lyon le boursier	Lyon the pursser
A boursses et alloyeres.	Hath pursses and pautners
Et les achattent les enfans	And them bye the chyldren.
Des tasses bien ouuries	Of the powches well wrought.
Lucie le bastarde	Lucie the bastarde
Ne fera iamais bien	Shall neuer doo well.
Car elle dist mal de ceulx	For she saith euyll of them
Qui bien luy ont fait	That well haue don to her
m Artin le especier	m Artin the grocer.
Vent pluiseurs especes	Selleth many spyces
De toutes manieres de pouldre.	Of all maners of poudre.
Pour faire les brouets	For to make browettys
Et a moult de boistes pointes.	And hath many boxes paynted
Plaines de confections	Full of confections

CAXTON'S FRENCH-ENGLISH PRIMER

18

William Caxton, *Doctrine to learn French and English.*
(Vocabulary in French and English)

Westminster: William Caxton, [*c.* 1480]
[26] leaves. 2°. 211 x 149 mm.

Provenance: various inscriptions of the Harrington family from Ridlington in Rutland dating from the 16th and 17th centuries.

Bamburgh Select 83

About four years after introducing printing to England, with nearly forty titles to his credit already, William Caxton published the present volume. The sheets of paper are slightly larger than those he normally used, no doubt because of the need for two columns, of French and English respectively. The book announces that it offers 'Ryght good lernyng./ For to lerne./ Shortly frenssh and englyssh'. More specifically, it advertises its value to merchants: 'Who this booke shall wylle lerne/ May well entreprise or take on honde/ Marchandises fro one land to anothir'. The text is translated from a version of *Le livre des mestiers*, a work composed in the fourteenth century probably by a school-master in Bruges, who translated French phrases into Flemish. Caxton, a mercer, was resident in Bruges for many years and from 1462 to 1470 was Governor of the English Nation there before embarking on his new career as a printer. This English translation is not by Caxton himself, but probably emanates from the commercial community in Flanders to which he had belonged. Types of coinage mentioned suggest 1465–6 as the date of the revised French version and the translation.

The vocabulary is organised under topics, which are listed at the beginning: suitable forms of greeting, birds, animals, trees, food and drink, the hierarchy of the Church and the state, merchandise and important fairs etc. The longest section gives proper names arranged in alphabetical order, to which in most cases the name of a trade is attached. So for example, 'Lyeuyn the brewar/ Breweth so much ale./ That he may not selle it'. In spite of the layout in short lines, the vocabulary is not simply organised as a list; the author addresses the reader in the first person and builds his enumeration of terms into passages of instruction, dialogue or even sketchy narrative, with the obvious intention of building up useful vocabulary – as well as of entertaining: 'Lenard the thaccher/ Hath coverd my litell hous./ With straw and with reed/ The latthes that he bought./ Be nothyng worth'. The entry on Lewin the inefficient brewer continues 'For he is renomed/ Of evyll drynke./ So hym behoveth othirwhyle/ To cast to fore the hogges'.

If the English sometimes appears rather stilted, this is because the translator tends to retain the French word-order and structures, no doubt to help the learner to understand the French phrase. For example, how to speak to a servant: 'Margote prengne de l'argent/ Va a la boucherye/ Sy achates de le (sic) char' is rendered ' Margret take of the silver/ Goo to the flesshshamels./ Bye ther of the flessh', choosing the most literal translation of the French partitive articles. The French itself contains many errors of gender, agreement and spelling, suggesting that Caxton's compositor for this volume did not himself know the language. A conscientious reader would nevertheless be able to communicate quite extensively – given help with pronunciation. The genre seems to have been a profitable one, for two other London printers published comparable texts in the 1490s. As with many utilitarian books, few copies survive – only four and one fragment of this edition.

Jenny and Richard Britnell

Eusebius' *World History*, a Fifteenth-Century Edition

19

Eusebius of Caesarea, *Chronicon* (translated by Jerome, with his continuation to the year 381; further continued by Prosper of Aquitaine, Matthaeus Palmerius of Florence (to 1448) and Matthias Palmerius of Pisa (to 1481); edited by J.L. Santritter).

Venice: Erhard Ratdolt, 13 September 1483.
[182] leaves; 4° (228 × 163 mm). Binding: dark brown calf over wooden boards, fillets and strapwork panel rolls, Venetian, *c.* 1490.

Provenance: from the library of Martin Routh (Routh 53.C.15).

SR.2.C.11

Eusebius (d. *c.* 339–40), bishop of Caesarea in Palestine, was a prolific Greek Christian writer who has been called the father of church history; his most famous work is the *Ecclesiastical History* which describes the rise of the Christian Church from the apostolic age down to the early years of the fourth century. His *Chronicon*, an account of world history from the Creation to his own day, was initially compiled before 303. Notable for its attempt to establish a precise dating of significant events (thus the birth of Christ is ascribed to the 5199th year of the world), it remains an invaluable guide to the chronology of ancient Greece, Rome and Israel. Following a short first book which provides an epitome of the history of several nations, the bulk of the work consists of a series of synchronical tables listing rulers, wars, natural disasters, foundations of cities, Olympiads and other remarkable occurrences.

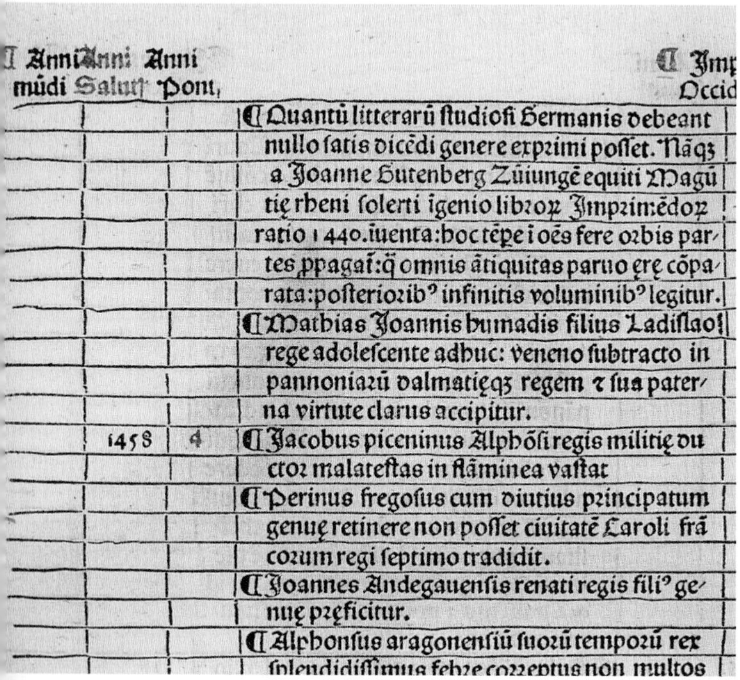
Anni Anni Anni
mūdi Saluti Pont,
Imp
Occid
Quantū litterarū studiosi Germanis debeant nullo satis dicēdi genere exprimi posset. Nāqz a Joanne Gutenberg Zūiungē equiti Magūtię rheni solerti igenio librorū Imprimēdorū ratio 1440. iuenta: hoc tēpe i oēs fere orbis partes ppagat: q̄ omnis ātiquitas paruo ęrę cōparata: posteriorib⁹ infinitis voluminib⁹ legitur.
Mathias Joannis huniadis filius Ladislao rege adolescente adhuc: veneno subtracto in pannoniarū dalmatięqz regem ⁊ sua paterna virtute clarus accipitur.
1458 4 Jacobus piceninus Alphōsi regis militię ductor malatestas in flāminea vastat
Perinus fregosus cum diutius principatum genuę retinere non posset ciuitatē Caroli frācorum regi septimo tradidit.
Joannes Andegauensis renati regis fili⁹ genuę pręficitur.
Alphonsus aragonensiū suorū temporū rex splendidissimus febre correptus non multos

In this its second but best fifteenth-century edition, Eusebius' work appears in the Latin translation of St Jerome (d. 420). On the opening page, reproduced here, Jerome begins with a call to copyists of books to take great care in their work (a piece of advice which might equally be applied to typesetters), before commenting on the difficulties of translating from one language to another.

The book was produced by Erhard Ratdolt, a native of Augsburg who migrated to Venice in 1476, where over the next decade he produced some of the finest Venetian incunabula. Returning to his home town around 1486, he continued his career as a printer there until his death, probably in 1528. In Venice Ratdolt displayed a penchant for printing historical, astronomical and mathematical works, which included the first edition of Euclid's *Elements* (1482). His books are elegantly printed, often (as here) in black and red, and are specially noted for their beautiful woodcut initial letters and page-borders, which were frequently imitated by other workshops. The *Chronicon*, most of which is set out in tabular form, is a striking example of Ratdolt's characteristically innovative and daring press-work.

Under the date 1457 occurs an early naming in print of Johann Gutenberg as the inventor of printing, the discovery being assigned to the year 1440. The chronicler adds that the art has subsequently spread over almost the entire world, so that the whole of antiquity can now be purchased cheaply and will be read by our descendants in countless volumes.

Geoffrey Scarre

EVSEBII CAESARIENSIS EPISCOPI CHRONICON ID EST TEMPORVM BREVIARIVM INCIPIT FOELICI/TER: QVEM HIERONYMVS PRAESBITER DIVINO EIVS INGENIO LATINVM FACERE CVRAVIT: ET VSQVE IN Valentē Cęsarem Romano Adiecit Eloquio. Quē ET Prosper deinde Matheꝰ palmeriꝰ Qui ea quę cōsecuta sūt adiicere curauere eidē postpositi subsequunt. At primū Hieronymi in huiꝰ codicis aliquādo descriptores ut archetypus describat adiuratio.

VERBA DIVI LITTERARVM PRINCIPIS HIERONYMI

ADiuro te quicūq; hos descripseris libros p̱ dominū nostrū iesū christū et gloriosū eius aduentū: in quo ueniet iudicare uiuos & mortuos ut cōferas quod scripseris & emēdes ad exēplaria ea de quibꝰ scripseris diligenter. Et hoc adiuratiōis genus transcribas & transferas in eum codicem quem descripseris.

Chronica Eusebii Hieronymi Incipit.

Prefatio Hieronymi

EVsebius Hieronymus Vincentio & Galieno suis Salutem. Vetus iste disertorum mos fuit ut exercendi ingenii causa gręcos libros latino sermone absoluerēt. Et quod plus ī se difficultatis habet poemata illustriū uirorū addita metri necessitate transferrēt. Vnde & noster Tulius Platonis integros libros ad uerbū interprętatus est. Et cū Aratū iā Romanū hexametris uersibꝰ edidisset in xenophontis economico lusit. In quo opere ita sępe aureū illud flumē eloquētię quibusdā scabris & turbulētis obicibꝰ retardatur ut qui interprętata nesciūt a Cicerone dicta nō credāt. Difficile est enī alienas linguas insequentē nō alicubi excidere arduū: ut quę in aliena lingua bene dicta sunt: eundē decorē in translatione cōseruēt. Significatū est aliquid unius uerbi proprietate nō habeo meū quo id efficiā: & dum quero implere sententiā longo ambitu

OCEANVS OCCIDENTALIS
MARE ATLANTICVM
SINVS HESPERIVS
CLIMA 1
CLIMA 2
CLIMA 3
CLIMA 7
DACIA
LIBYA
INTERIOR
AETHIOPIA INTERIOR
AEGYPTO
SVB
AETHIOPIA
ARABIA
FELIX
SINVS
SINVS BARBARICVS
5
10
15
20
25
30
35
40
45
50
55
60
65
70
75
80
85

An Early Printed Map of Britain

20

Ptolemy, *Geographia.*

Rome: Pietro de la Torre, 1490.

[114] leaves. 2°. 415 x 270 mm.

Provenance: Italian ?17th-century library stamp; from the collection of Martin Routh (Routh 60.A.12).

SR. 2.C.2

Ptolemy (Claudius Ptolemaeus) lived in Alexandria in the second century AD. Among his scientific works, written in Greek, is a treatise on geography, a detailed description of the world that includes the coordinates – the latitude and longitude – of some 5,000 places. From these coordinates, maps could be made, though whether Ptolemy himself did this is open to doubt. From the thirteenth century onwards, copies of the Greek text include maps – one of the world and either twenty-six or (with modified text) sixty-four regional ones – but they may well have been constructed by Byzantine map-makers.

Before the fifteenth century the work was known only in the Greek-speaking world of the eastern empire; however, around 1406 Jacopo d'Angelo at Rome produced a Latin translation, making it accessible to western Europe. An immediate success, it was often copied in the course of the fifteenth century. Besides the map of the world and the twenty-six or sixty-four regional maps, a few copies also include new maps of particular regions. The Ptolemy maps contributed significantly to western Europe's developing interest in cartography. The calculation of new tables of coordinates by mathematicians in Austria; the extension of the so-called portolan sea-charts beyond the Mediterranean and west European coastlines to include the Atlantic islands and the newly-explored west African coast; a new, if modest, output of local maps in some parts of Europe; the books of islands (descriptions and maps of the islands of the Aegean) – these were all steps leading to the cartographic revolution of the sixteenth century when, throughout Europe, maps started to become objects of everyday use.

It is unsurprising that Ptolemy's treatise should be among the earliest books to be printed. It was first published at Vicenza in 1475 without illustrations, but editions with maps followed from Bologna (1477), Rome (1478 and 1490) and Ulm (1482 and 1486). Durham possesses a superb copy of the edition published at Rome by Pietro de la Torre, whose colophon gives the exact date: 4 November 1490. The maps of the world and twenty-six regions are placed at the end of Ptolemy's text, preceding a separate geographical work, 'De locis et mirabilibus mundi', that is appended to it. They were printed from copper plates – two for each map – that had been produced for the 1478 edition under the direction of Conrad Sweynheym, one of the pioneers of copper-plate engraving in Italy. The letters and numbers were punched, not engraved, on the plates.

Illustrated overleaf is the map of Britain and Ireland. The elongation of northern Scotland towards the east is characteristic of Ptolemy maps and reappears on other maps of Britain until the late sixteenth century.

P. D. A. Harvey

·PRIMA · EVROPĘ ·

·VNVS·GRADVS·LONGITVDINIS·IN·HOC·PARALELLO·PER·
·THILEN·HABET·MILIARIA·25 $\frac{5}{8}$·STADIA·VERO·225·

·DIFFERENTIA·PARTIS·SVPERIORIS·AD·INFER·
·IOREM·TABVLĘ·IN·STADIIS·QVIDEM·2590·
·IN·MILIARIBVS·AVTEM·240·

·MILIARIA·36 $\frac{1}{2}$·

·VNVS·GRADVS·LONGITVDINIS
·CONTINET·STADIA·317·ET·
·MILIARIA·38·

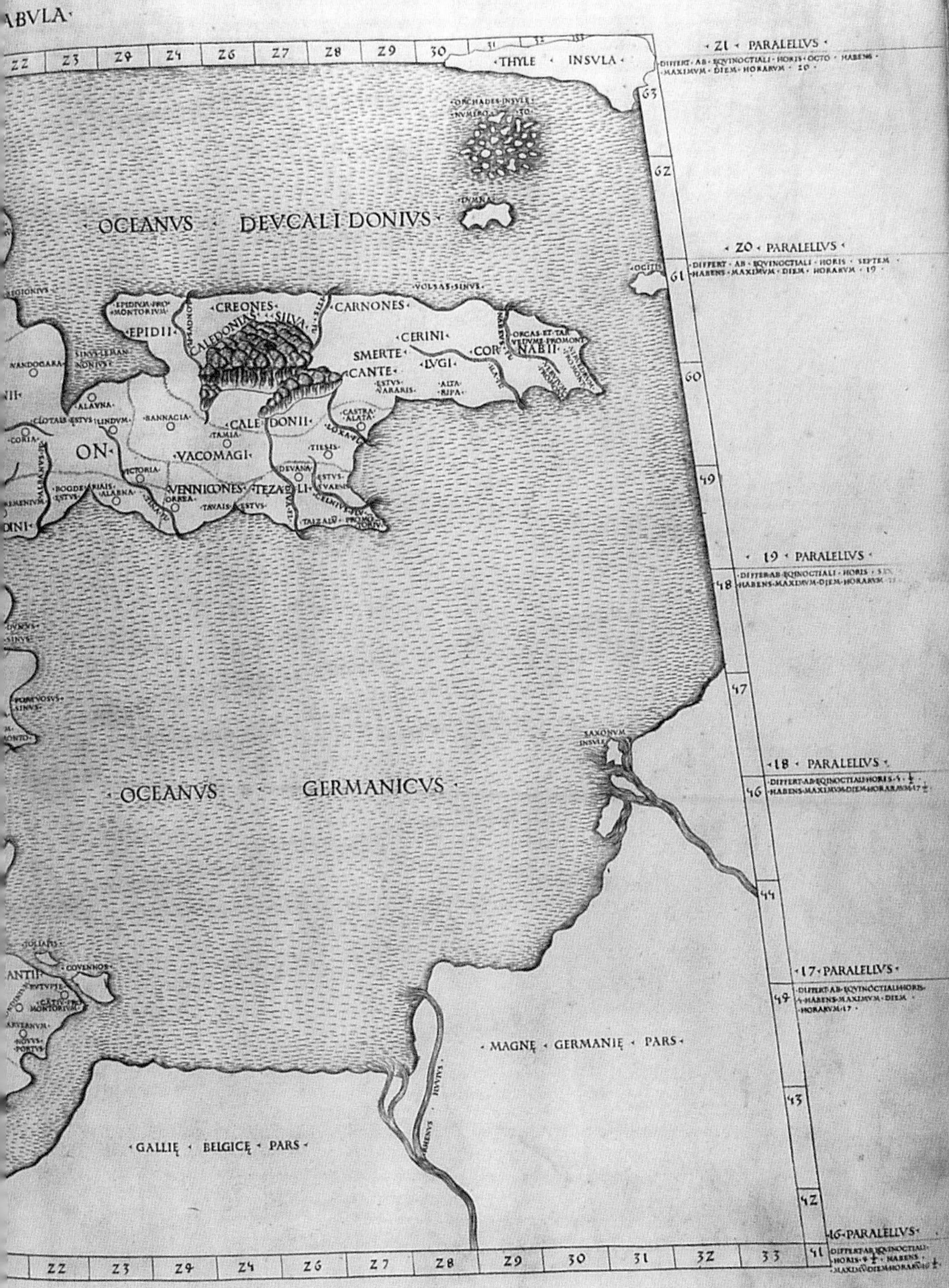
ABVLA·
THYLE · INSVLA ·
OCEANVS · DEVCALIDONIVS ·
CREONES
CALEDONIA SILVA
CARNONES
EPIDII
CERINI
SMERTE
CANTE
LVGI
CORNABII
CALEDONII
VACOMAGI
VENNICONES
TEZALI
ON
OCEANVS · GERMANICVS ·
MAGNĘ · GERMANIĘ · PARS ·
GALLIĘ · BELGICĘ · PARS ·
· 21 · PARALELLVS ·
· 20 · PARALELLVS ·
· 19 · PARALELLVS ·
· 18 · PARALELLVS ·
· 17 · PARALELLVS ·
16 · PARALELLVS ·
22 23 24 25 26 27 28 29 30 31 32 33
63 62 61 60 59 58 57 56 55 54 53 52 51

The Dance of Death

21

Hartmann Schedel, *Liber chronicorum.*

Nuremberg: Anton Koberger, 12 July 1493.
[20], CCXCIX, [7] leaves. 2°. 440 x 300 mm.

Provenance: inscriptions of Jehan Morisot and Edmond Morisot, 15th-17th century; armorial binding stamps of Léonor d'Estampes de Valencay as Bishop of Chartres cut from earlier binding; from Cosin's library (Cosin R.1.1).

SR.2.B.4

The World History of the Nuremberg physician and humanist Hartmann Schedel (d. 1513), published in 1493 by Anton Koberger, is one of the greatest of incunabula, and defined a new standard for illustrated printing. Not only does the book contain an unprecedented number of images (1,809 from 645 woodblocks), many of a grand scale, but its artwork is of a high quality: the design was entrusted to the workshop of Michael Wolgemut and Wilhelm Pleydenwurff, which then included the young Albrecht Dürer.

The illustration featured here shows the 'Totentanz' (Dance of Death) a common late medieval image. It depicts four dancing figures in various stages of decomposition, pipes being played to assist the movement. The accuracy of the depiction of the skeleton is limited (the ribs, for example, are incorrect in terms of number and shape, none of the skeletons has a real pelvis, and the drawings of some of the internal organs are also inaccurate) but it illustrates the anatomical knowledge of the time. A clear understanding of the skeleton had to wait until 1543 when Vesalius published the first real atlas of anatomy, *De humani corporis fabrica.* Nevertheless, the picture is a powerful one. Several similar caricatures of this period incorporate the figure of a doctor (identified by the piss-pot he holds), again emphasising the futility of trying to cheat death and the powerlessness of medicine. Such caricatures have similar skeletal outlines, often with worms, eyes hanging out, and degenerating muscles. In one picture the skeletal figure is depicted brandishing a bone (a femur) above his head in defiance.

Such images were often associated with poems. This one is from the Marian Church in Berlin.

Death (to Doctor)

Good Doctor, Master of your art
Thrice have I called you to depart
Your life continues on and on
When to God you should have gone
Put down your glass, let us away
My dance to you let me display.

Doctor (to Death)

All-powerful God hear now my cry
For my urine does not lie
I must to the apothec'ry
For death he stands in front of me
No ointment can improve my state
For Jesus now for me doth wait

The popularity of pictures and texts on the subject suggest several implications. The first is the inevitability of death and the difficulty of avoiding it. Indeed a narrative poem of the thirteenth century, the 'Dit des trois vifs et des trois morts' (the Exchange of the three living and the three dead), like the much earlier and widely-diffused 'Dry bones speak' homiletic topos (where the dead warn the living of their inescapable fate), demonstrate the long lineage of such ideas.

The second is that death is a great leveller; no matter who you are or what your status, death equalises everything. It is recorded that in October 1424 in the Cimetière des Innocents at Paris in the presence of the Duke of Burgundy, real dances were in fact held pointing out the obvious implications of death. However this was viewed less as a warning against the dangers of sin, rather as a call to enjoy life at the present – it will end all too soon. The quality of life and its enjoyment, here and now, was perhaps the main message.

Kenneth Calman

Imago mortis

Morte nihil melius. vita nil peius iniqua
O p̄ma mors hoīm. reqes eterna laborū
Tu senile iugum domino volente relaxas
Vinctorūq3 graues adimis ceruice cathenas
Exiliumq3 leuas. 7 carceris hostia frangis
Eripis indignis. iusti bona ptibus equans
Atq3 immota manes. nulla exorabilis arte
A primo prefixa die. tu cuncta quieto
Ferre iubes animo. promisso fine laborum
Te sine supplicium. vita est carcer perennis

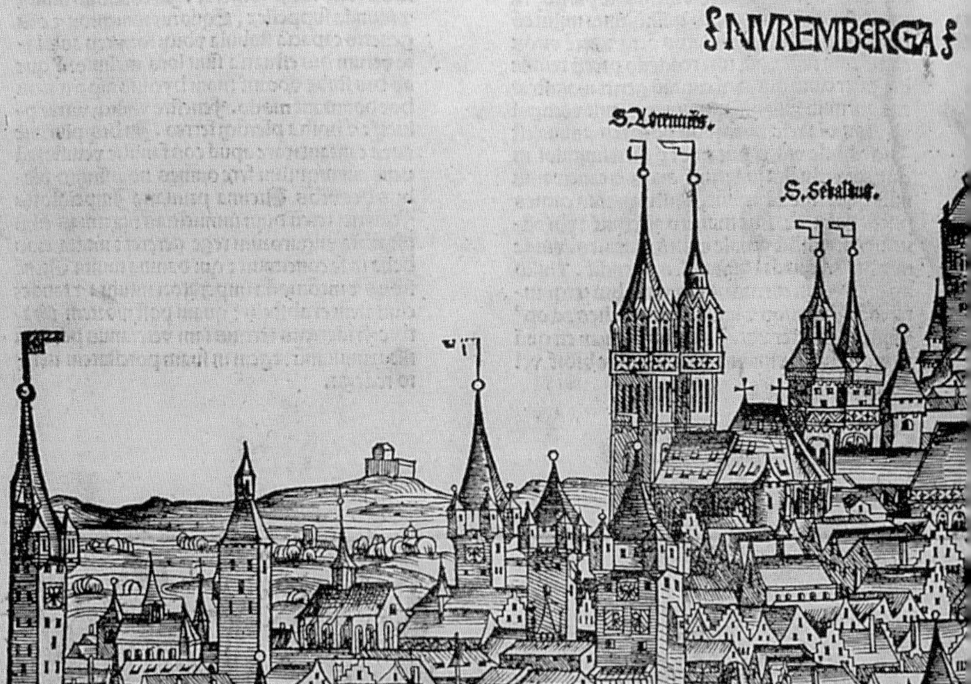
NVREMBERGA
S.Sebaldus.

Religion for the Laity

22

The abbaye of the holy Ghost.

Westminster: Wynkyn de Worde, [*c.* 1497]
[40] p. 4°. 180 x 125 mm. STC 13609.

Provenance: unknown before Bamburgh Castle Library

Bamburgh Select 101

Among the riches of the Bamburgh collection are fifteen short religious pieces dated 1496–1516 (Bamburgh Select 98–112); previously forming a single volume, they were rebound separately about a century ago. Four of them are unique, most survive in just two or three copies and only one reaches double figures: John Fisher's *Mornynge remembraunce ... of Margarete Countesse of Rychemonde*. Margaret Beaufort, Countess of Richmond and Derby (d. 1509), was a significant patron of Wynkyn de Worde (d. 1535) who printed all but two of these tracts.

After Caxton's death in 1492 de Worde took over his premises, types, woodcuts and even his 'W C' printer's device (see p. 23). But he also introduced italic type into England and pioneered the printing of music from movable type in Higden's *Polychronicon*, 1495 (Bamburgh Select 13).

De Worde's religious publications were more numerous and diverse than Caxton's had been and most, like the Bamburgh tracts, were published in the smaller, cheaper quarto size. They included works for professed religious: John Alcock's two sermons and translations of the rules of SS. Francis and Augustine. For parochial clergy there were translations from John Pecham's Provincial Constitutions, *Exornatorium Curatorum*. But far more significant was de Worde's recognition of the increasing numbers of devout and literate layfolk, amongst others, who wanted devotional material made available in English. Betson's *Ryght profytable treatyse* was 'medefull to religious people as to the laye people'.

The devotional works in the Bamburgh tracts were suited to any reader. Some had circulated in manuscript versions for many years: familiarity and accessibility were valued more highly than originality. The constituent parts of *The abbaye of the holy Ghost* – the foundation charter, the story of the Fall, the Council of Heaven, the description of Christ's life and death, the occasional flights of contemplative language (one image reminiscent of Julian of Norwich), and the final Harrowing of Hell – would all have been familiar from other treatises, homilies, drama and art. Although the basic image was of a religious community, that community of virtues was founded in the conscience of the individual, scattered by the Fall and recovered in the course of Christ's life and death.

De Worde rarely published a book without illustration. Caxton's woodcut of the Crucifixion used on the back of the *Abbaye's* title-page occurs in four other Bamburgh tracts. However, the title-page illustration of the *Abbaye* might well have puzzled more alert readers: the three Persons of the Trinity and the four Daughters of God (Mercy, Truth, Justice and Peace; Psalm 85); but why the angel? Gabriel has no place in the Council of Heaven as described in the *Abbaye*; however, he takes a crucial role in the Council that opens the *Speculum Vitae Christi* and this woodcut was taken over from Caxton's two editions of that work – convenient rather than accurate.

This combination of clear visual images and the retelling of Salvation History in a way that was both personal and communal, accessible and memorable, was well suited to the increasing numbers of readers who lacked formal academic skills and theological training.

J. T. Rhodes

¶ The abbaye of the holy Ghost.

ARISTOPHANES, THE FIRST PRINTED EDITION

23

Aristophanes, *Comoediae novem.*

Venice : Aldus Manutius, 15 July 1498.

[348] leaves. 2°. 320 x 230 mm.

Provenance: given to Martin Routh by William Andrew Jenner (1751?–1832) (Routh 21.B.4).

SR. 2.D.11

Because of the typographical challenges and restricted audience, the printing of Greek texts lagged behind that of Latin ones. Credit for remedying the situation belongs to Aldus Manutius (*c.* 1450–1515) who established a press at Venice (the major centre of early printing in Italy: cf. no. 19) that specialized in Greek works, and between 1495 and 1515 published first editions of many of the major Greek authors. The texts were not cheap – the present item, when new, cost two and a half gold pieces – but editorial standards were often high.

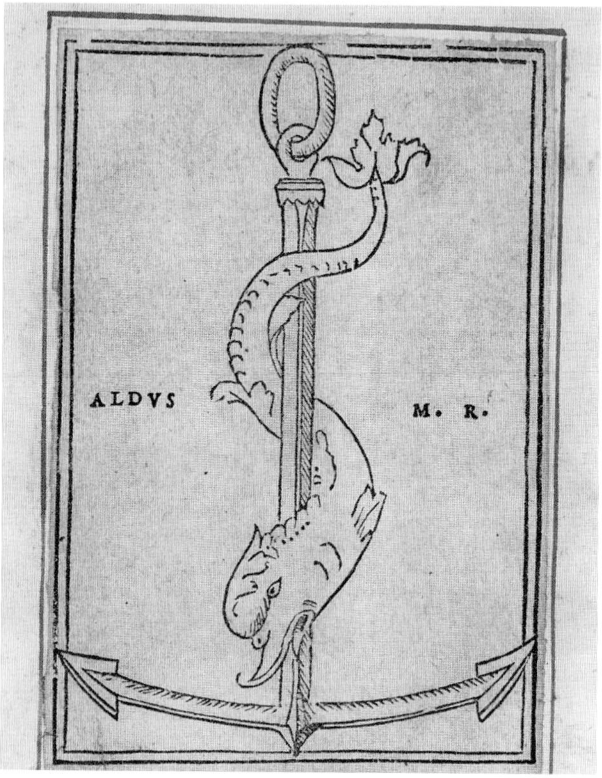

Aldus' editor for his text of the comic playwright Aristophanes (d. early fourth century BC) was the Cretan, Marcus Musurus (*c.* 1470–1517) – a man whose subsequent penchant for lecturing in Padua at 7.00 a.m. in the depths of winter apparently deterred all but the elderly professor of Latin from coming to hear him. The Aldine edition is free from many of the defects common in most of the medieval manuscripts, although it is clear that Musurus was for the most part simply accepting revisions made earlier by the Byzantine, Demetrius Triclinius. His own awareness of Classical Greek usage and metre has been characterized as 'fitful', but he did bring a semblance of order to the scholia (explanatory material preserved in the margins of the manuscripts) – a labour dogged by printers' errors, which he picturesquely compares to dealing with the heads of the mythological Hydra. Whatever its limitations, the Aldine edition was not fully superseded until the work of Brunck (1783) and Bekker (1829) centuries later.

Apart from the interest of the text, the Aldine Aristophanes includes a notable editor's preface. Musurus commends Aristophanes for his style and vocabulary; the reader who takes care to imitate him in conversation may win a reputation for having been brought up in Greece itself. Indeed, Aristophanes will be welcome to the good folk of Venice through his depiction of classical Athens, of which Venice is in some ways a copy. He also offers a pleasant change from Aristotle (Aldus had issued a five-volume set of Aristotle and Theophrastus over the previous three years). This preface is itself a rich document for cultural history, shedding light upon the appropriation of classical models (Venice as Athens), linguistic aspiration (the implicit desirability of being able to speak like a classical Athenian), and the classics as a means to self-improvement.

L. V. Pitcher

ἈΡΙΣΤΟΦΆΝΟΥΣ, ΠΛΟΥ͂ΤΟΣ.

⊢ Καρίων οἰκέτης.

ΩΣ ἀργαλέον πρᾶγμ᾽ ἐστὶν
ὦ Ζεῦ καὶ θεοί
Δοῦλον γενέσθαι παραφρονοῦν-
τος δεσπότου.
Ἢν γὰρ τὰ βέλτισθ᾽ ὁ θεράπων
λέξας τύχῃ,
Δόξῃ δὲ μὴ δρᾶν ταῦτα τῷ κεκτημένῳ,
Μετέχειν ἀνάγκη τὸν θεράποντα τῶν κακῶν.
Τοῦ σώματος γὰρ οὐκ ἐᾷ τὸν κύριον
Κρατεῖν ὁ δαίμων, ἀλλὰ τὸν ἐωνημένον.
Καὶ ταῦτα μὲν δὴ, ταῦτα. τῷ δὲ Λοξίᾳ

⊢ Ὡς ἀργαλέον. ὁ θεράπων δυσφορεῖ τῷ δεσπότου ἑπομένου τυφλῷ ἀνδρί. τοῦ δὲ ὡς, πέπλεκται ἡ διάνοια, ἐκ τοῦ θαυμαστικοῦ καὶ σχετλιασμοῦ. τὸ γὰρ ὡς ἐπίρρημα, ἐστὶν ἀμφοτέρων. ἢ ἐνταῦθα εἴληπται, ὡς τὸ τάσεως δηλωτικόν. ἐπαυξάνει δὲ οὐ δι᾽ αἰτίαν μάχην, ἀλλὰ διὰ τὸ ἐπαχθὲς τῶν δεσποτῶν. τὸ δὲ ἀργαλέον, χαλεπόν. δύσκολον. δυσχερές. εἴρηται δὲ παρὰ τὸ ἄλγος, ἀλγαλέον. καὶ κατὰ τροπὴν τοῦ λ εἰς ρ. ὡς τὸ δαλγία κεδαργία. ἢ ἔργον παρὰ τοῖς παλαιοῖς, τὸ δυσχερές. ἐκ τούτου παράγωγον ἀργαλέον. ὡς ἀπὸ τοῦ ἐπῶ ἀπύω.

Ὦ Ζεῦ. τὸν δία παρέλαβε κατ᾽ ἐξοχὴν τῶν ἄλλων θεῶν ὥς τὸ, Ζεὺς δ᾽ ἐπεὶ οὖν Τρῶάς τε καὶ Ἕκτορα νηυσὶ πέλασσε. καὶ ὅλως τὸν Ἕκτορα ὀνομάζων, κατ᾽ ἐξοχὴν παρείληφε. Δοῦλον γενέσθαι. χαλεποῦ ὄντος φύσει τοῦ δουλεύειν, χαλεπώτερον γίνεται, ἐὰν ἀνοήτῳ τις δεσπότῃ ὑπηρετῇ. Μὴ δρᾶν ταῦτα. οἱ γράφοντες ταυτά, οὐ καλῶς γράφουσιν. εὕρηται γὰρ ἐν πολλοῖς τῶν παλαιῶν ἀντιγράφων τὸ ταῦτα. καὶ ἔστι κρεῖττον ἐκείνου. Μετέχειν ἀνάγκη. πρὸς τὸ ποιητικόν. Ἥμισυ γάρ τ᾽ ἀρετῆς ἀπαμείρεται εὐρύοπα Ζεὺς Ἀνέρος, εὖτ᾽ ἄν μιν κατὰ δούλιον ἦμαρ ἕλῃσι. τί γὰρ κακώτερον τοῦ τὰ ἐναντία ἑαυτῷ διαπράττεσθαι τίμια, ἐν τῷ μὴ πείθειν ἃ βούλεται, καὶ διὰ τὴν ἄλλων ἀφροσύνης ἀνέχεσθαι. Τῶν κακῶν. τῆς ἀφροσύνης ὧν ὁ δεσπότης ἔχει. ἤγουν τῶν πληγῶν, ἃς τοῖς ἀπειθοῦσι τοῖς δεσπόταις ὀφείλονται. εἰώθασι δὲ οἱ ἀττικοὶ τὰ ἄρθρα πλεονάζειν. ὥσπερ οὖν ἐν τῷ, τὰ βέλτιστα περισσὸν ἦν ἀττικῶς τὸ ἄρθρον, οὕτω κἀνταῦθα τὸ τῶν. ἐν τοῖς ἑξῆς τό, τὸ ὡς ἐν τῷ τὸ ποῖον. τὸ δὲ ταῦτα τὸ δεύτερον, ἀλλ᾽ ἔστιν ἀντὶ τοῦ ταυτὶ ὡς οἷον ταυτί πως. ἀλλ᾽ αὖ τί τοῦ ταῦτα πάλιν ἀττικῶς. Τοῦ σώματος γάρ. οἷον αὐτὸν ἑαυτοῦ τὸν δοῦλον οὐκ ἐᾷ κρατεῖν. μάλιστα γὰρ κύριος τοῦ σώματος ἕκαστος αὐτὸς ἑαυτοῦ. Τὸν ἐωνημένον. ἀντὶ τοῦ τὸν ὠνησάμενον ἀπὸ τοῦ ὠνοῦμαι. λέγουσι γὰρ διὰ τῆς αὐτῆς φωνῆς τὰς τοῦ ῥήματος κλίσεις. τοῦ δὲ ὀνόματος τὸ πληθυντικὸν οὐκ ἔστιν ὠνησάμενοι. διὸ μεταβαλόντες αὐτὸ ἐπὶ ἑτέραν φωνὴν πριάμενοι λέγουσιν ἀττικοί. Καὶ ταῦτα μὲν δὴ ταῦτα. καὶ ταῦτα μὲν δὴ τοῦτον ἔχει τὸν τρόπον. ἔστι δὲ τὸ σχῆμα ἀποθετικὸν τῆς πρώτης διανοίας. Τῷ δὲ Λοξίᾳ. τῷ Ἀπόλλωνι. ἤτοι τῷ λοξὰ ἵεν πέμποντι. λοξὰ γὰρ μαντεύεται ὁ θεός. ἢ τῷ λοξὴν πορείαν ποιουμένῳ. ὁ αὐτὸς γάρ ἐστι τῷ ἡλίῳ.

A Unique but Flawed English Book of Hours

24

Hours (Sarum Use).

[London: Richard Pynson, c. 1500]

Two damaged paper sheets of c. 360x295 mm, folded to make pages of 155 x 104 mm (text-block: 100 x 75 mm). STC 15893.

Provenance: re-used in the ?English binding of a copy of Boniface *Liber sextus decretalium* published in Lyon in 1507 (SB+ 0072).

SR.3.A.22

These sheets represent two quires from a Book of Hours. The thirty-two pages printed thereon contain the Hours of the Virgin from Prime (the first daytime office) to Compline (the last office of the day), plus concluding Marian devotions (e.g. *Salve regina, Gaudes*), breaking off in the prayer, *O intemerata*. The text follows the Use of Sarum, the dominant English form at the time, complete with elements from the Hours of the Cross. These pages would normally have been preceded by a calendar and by the Offices of Matins and Lauds, this last probably including Suffrages (devotions to saints).

Books of Hours (Primers) were relatively common in late medieval and Tudor England, owned by a broad cross-section of literate, even semi-literate, lay-folk. During the half-century following the first printing of a Sarum Hours (by Caxton, c. 1476), some 100 editions are known to have been produced. Yet owing, on the one hand, to regular use, and, on the other, to the impact of the Reformation – the official royal Primer of 1545 was supposed to supersede all previous copies, which were further imperilled by legislation against superstitious books and images five years later – many of the earliest editions are now known only from fragments.

Our pages are associated with Richard Pynson (*c.* 1449–1529/30), England's principal printer after Wynkyn de Worde, following the death of Caxton. Of Norman origin, Pynson had moved to London by 1482, and was in the book-trade by 1490; the earliest known publication bearing his imprint is dated 1492 – the year after Caxton's death. A decade later he was based in Fleet Street, specialising in legal printing; he achieved the status of 'King's Printer' by 1506, and within six years secured a monopoly on the publication of statutes of the realm.

Alongside legal texts, Pynson also produced common – hence marketable – liturgical books of different classes, ranging from fine missals literally fit for a king (Henry VII, in 1504) to Hours for the modest purse. A contract reveals that his print-run for an edition of such texts could be 600. While competition within England was limited, foreign printers were a force to be reckoned with: of the twenty-nine editions of Sarum Hours known up to 1500, only twelve were English, while fifteen were French, with one each from Antwerp and Venice. Equally, in the decade before Henry VIII forbad the importation of copies (1538), a single Parisian publisher, François Regnault, issued nearly thirty editions for the English market.

The principal book of lay devotion, Hours, even economically-printed ones, generally included decoration. The artwork in early English printing was, on the whole, less accomplished than that on the Continent, and our item is no exception. Compact woodcuts of elementary workmanship and conventional iconography mark the major divisions of the text. There are three examples on each sheet: the Coronation of the Virgin (for Terce), the Nativity (for Sext), and the Flight into Egypt (for None) appear on the first; while on the second are a duplicate of the Flight (this time for Vespers), the instruments of the passion plus Mary (for Compline), and finally a smaller Virgin and Child (for *Salve regina*). The relationship of subject-matter to text here is idiosyncratic, but printers could be surprisingly careless in such matters. They also regularly re-used blocks (cf. no. 22), even within one publication. Nevertheless, the duplication of the Flight for sequential Offices, but two folios apart, is jarring. As these texts appeared on different sheets, the anomaly may not have been apparent during production; but that it would then rapidly have been identified as unfortunate can hardly be doubted. Although, as noted, many editions of printed Hours are now represented only by fragments, these oddities, when taken in conjunction with the fact that our sheets were recycled as binding material within a decade or so, suggest that they were trials or rejects – providing insight into the practicalities and pitfalls of early printing.

Richard Gameson

6b

stoꝝ ut nõ extendant iusti ad iniq̃tatē
manus suas. Benefac dñe bonis ⁊ rectis
corde. Declinantes aũt i obligationes
adducet dñs cũ opantib⁹ iniq̃tatē pax
sup israel. Gl'ia. ãn. Rubuȝ quē viderat
moyses inconbustũ ꝯseruatã agnouim⁹ tuã
laudabilē virginitatē dei genitrix intercede
p nobis. Capitulum.
Et sic in syõ firmata sũ ⁊ in ciui
tate sanctificata similiter req̃eui ⁊ in ie
rusalē potestas mea. Deo gracias. Post
partũ virgo inuiolata pmãsisti Post partũ
V. Dei genitrix intercede p nobis Inuiola
ta pmansisti. Gloria Post partũ. V. Speci
osa facta es ⁊ suauis. R. In deliciis tuis sã
cta dei genitrix Domine exaudi Et clamor
Concede nos famul' vt supra
Hora sexta ies⁹ ē cruci ꝯclauatus

3a

Quia p sãctã crucē. ⁊c. Dñe iesu xpe. ⁊c.
Hora prima dña vidēs flagella
tũ suũ vnigenitũ turpiter tra
ctatum Colaphis ⁊ alapis sputo defor
matũ. Manus torquēs grauiter ruit i
ploratũ. V. Te laudam⁹. R. Ut intendas
Oratio. Domine scē iesu fili dulcis
virginis. ⁊c. vt supra.

Deus in adiuto
riũ meũ intēde
Dñe ad adiu
uandũ me festi
na Gl'a patri
Sicut erat. al
leluya Himn⁹
Ueni creator
spiritus. ⁊c.

2b

sine semine largit⁹ ē nobis suã deitatē. Ca
In oibus requiē quesiui ⁊ in he
reditate dñi morabor tũc prece
pit ⁊ dixit michi creator oim qui crea
uit me req̃euit i tabernaculo meo. Deo
gratias. R. Aue maria gratia plena domi
nu s tecũ. Aue maria. Benedita tu in mulie
ribus ⁊ benedictus fructus vētris tui Dñs
tecũ. Gloria patri ⁊ filio: ⁊ spiritui sancto.
Aue maria. Sancta dei genitrix virgo sēp
maria. Intercede p nobis ad dñm deũ no
strũ. Dñe exaudi orationē meã ⁊ clamor me
us ad te veniat. Or. Concede nos. vts.
Hora prima duct⁹ est ies⁹ ad py
latũ. Falsis testimoniis multũ
accusatũ. In collo pcutiũt manibus li
gatũ vultũ dei ꝯspuũt lumē celi gratũ:
Adoramus te xpe ⁊ benedicim⁹ tibi. R.

7a

Atq₃ cũ latroib⁹ pendēs deputat⁹ Pre
tormētis sitiēs felle saturat⁹. Agn⁹ cri
mē diluit sic ludificat⁹ Adora. Dñe. ⁊c
Hora sexta respicit mater suum
natũ. Obstitũ vulnerib⁹ i cru
ce leuatũ. Int' fures positũ felleq₃ pota
tũ Illa secũ sēcies red dit eiulatũ. Te lau
dam⁹. Oro. Domine scē iesu vt supra

Ad Nonam

Deus in
adiuto
riũ meũ intēde
Dñe ad adiu
uandũ me festi
na: Gloria.
Sicut Hymnus. Ueni cre
ator spũs ps

T M
THEODRIC MARTIN

25

The First Edition of *Utopia*

Thomas More, *Utopia*.

[Louvain]: arte Theodorici Martini ... typographi almae Louaniensium Academiae, [1516].

[108]p. 4°. 250 x 140 mm. Binding: early 16th-century blind-tooled calf.

Provenance: marginal annotations and 'index' in 16th-century continental hand. Final leaf has indecipherable ownership inscriptions of a 16th-century canon of ?Corbeil. Possibly acquired by John Cosin when in exile in France, 1644–60 (Cosin W.5.32).

SB 0300

Given its lasting political and cultural resonances, and the mountain of writing that it has inspired, the first edition of More's *Utopia* impresses us initially by its physical slightness. The most dramatic events of the author's life – his grappling with heresy in the wake of Luther's rebellion, the 'Great Matter' of Henry VIII's divorce, More's Lord Chancellorship, trial for treason, and martyrdom – all lay in the future. Yet the handsomely-tooled boards of this slim *libellus* (a mere 52 leaves in a small quarto format) contain in an aesthetic equilibrium some powerful opposing forces. The title-page calls attention to More's Englishness (a 'citizen' of London), but the para-texts (map, alphabet, epigram, 'authenticating' letters) reinforce his place within the pan-European Republic of Letters (*respublica litterarum*). More had travelled to Flanders the previous year (1515) in the company of Cuthbert Tunstall, future bishop of Durham (1530). His distance from London and his introduction (through Erasmus) to a wider circle of continental humanists allowed him in *Utopia* to marry an (often ironic) portrait of an apparently newly-discovered commonwealth (Book II) with an astringent critique of contemporary Europe in general, England in particular (Book I).

A Latin epigram on the second verso brings out a latent pun in the title – between two Greek words, *eu-topos* ('Good Place') and u-topos ('No Place'). This self-cancelling quality pervades the whole work. The map of Utopia shows a river called Ahydra ('without water'); the main speaker shares his first name with an archangel, Raphael ('God has healed' or 'God Heals' in Hebrew), but his surname (Hythlodaeus) means 'Dispenser of Nonsense'. Much in Utopia (especially Book II) is performative, an exercise in the Lucianic tradition of 'serious play' that bewildered so many of More's English contemporaries: proto-communism, euthanasia, the employment of mercenaries, the assassination of enemies, the ordination of women, and the expectation that prospective spouses see one another naked before betrothal, are all described by Hythlodaeus with apparent approval. The author himself maintains a studied ambivalence, with his persona (Morus) finally acknowledging that, while many aspects of Utopian society are manifestly absurd, he would like (but does not expect) to see certain (unspecified) Utopian practices adopted in Europe. If the conflicting vectors of More's work resolve themselves into any single direction, it may be this: the Utopians, relying on Reason alone, have built a society which, in some respects, is superior to any in Christendom; the nations of Europe, enjoying the benefits not merely of Reason but of Divine Revelation, have no excuse for not being better.

Further Latin editions of *Utopia* followed quickly (Paris, 1517; Basle, 1518; Florence, 1519) and the work was translated into German (1524), French (1530), Italian (1548), and English (1551). Its influence can be felt in works as different as Rabelais' *Gargantua* and Voltaire's *Candide*, and in a long train of Utopian and Dystopian fiction leading to Huxley's *Brave New World* and Atwood's *The Handmaid's Tale*.

Robert H. F. Carver

VTOPIAE INSVLAE FIGVRA

20597/2

Clarissimo D. Hieronymo Buslidio præposito Ariensi, Catholici regis Caroli a cõsiliis Petrus Aegidius Antuerpiensis S. D.

Vperioribus hisce diebus ornatissime

Alphabetum quod hic antecedebat, extat pag. seq.

Tetrastichon vernacula Vtopiensium lingua,

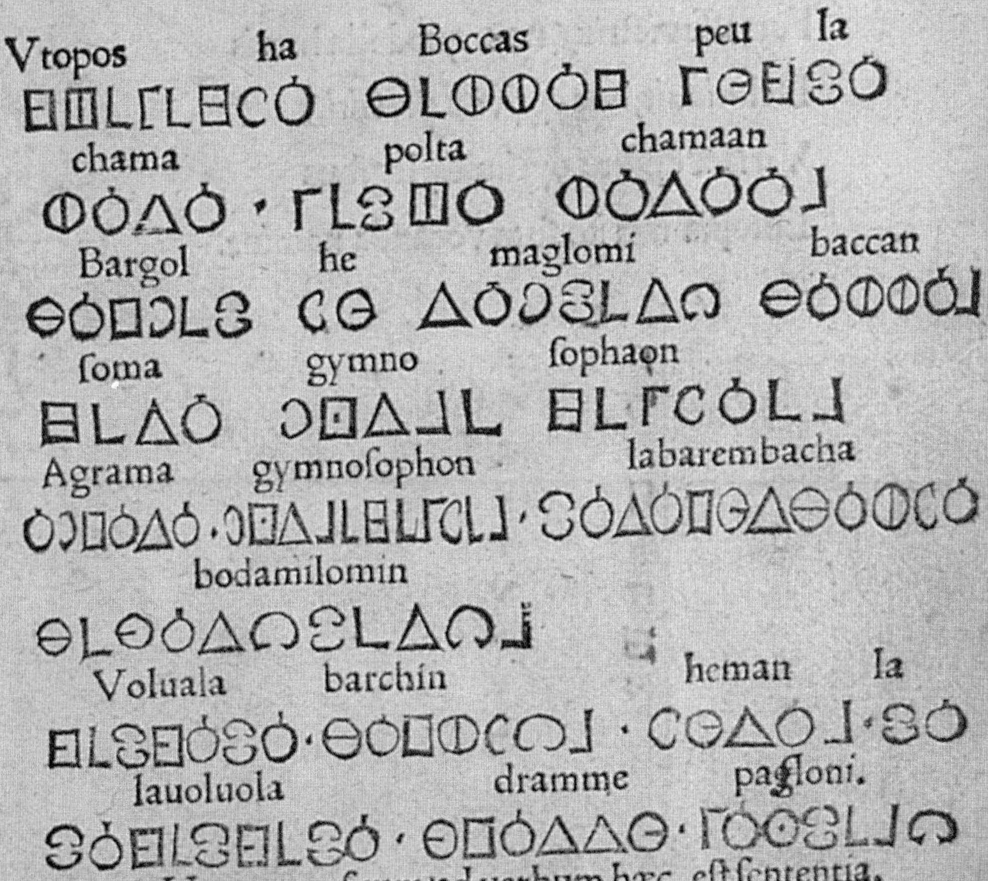

Vtopos ha Boccas peu la
chama polta chamaan
Bargol he maglomi baccan
soma gymno sophaon
Agrama gymnosophon labarembacha
bodamilomin
Voluala barchin heman la
lauoluola dramme pagloni.

Horum versuum ad verbum hæc est sententia.

Vtopus me dux ex non insula fecit insulam
Vna ego terrarum omnium absq; philosophia
Ciuitatem philosophicam expressi mortalibus
Libẽter impartio mea, nõ grauatim accipio meliora,

An Illuminated French Book of Hours 26

Heures

Paris: printed for Germain Hardouyn, [1520].
Parchment. [84] leaves. 8°. 175 x 70 mm.

Provenance: inscription of Vincent ?Soubray 1629; from the library of Martin Routh (Routh 17.D.1).

SB 0316

Books of Hours proliferated during the fifteenth and sixteenth centuries; as literacy increased, they gave lay-people the sort of direct and democratic access to God, the Virgin Mary, and the saints that had previously been the preserve of the priest and his breviary. The centrepiece of the Book of Hours is the Little Office of the Virgin Mary, accompanied by a rich selection of essentials for private reflection: a calendar of saints' days, an almanac for calculating the date of Easter, prayers to the saints, and the Office of the Dead. Printing made them widely available, less as the luxury objects that manuscripts had been than as tools, virtually mass-produced, for daily prayer. Printers like Germain Hardouyn – who advertises himself so flamboyantly on this page with his address ('between the two gates of the Palace, at the Sign of St Marguerite') – and his brother Gilles lived conveniently close to the royal palace on the Ile de la Cité; and for the luxury market they printed elegant Books of Hours with woodcuts meticulously hand-coloured. This copy is rather more modest: although printed on vellum, its pages are a little cramped, its images few and rather crudely coloured, the painted borders sketchy. Yet what we see on this opening shows that Germain had a particular market in mind.

The volume is in what is called the 'holster', or 'agenda', format which was sometimes used for small devotional books in France – slim and small enough to be slipped into a pocket or a bag. Precisely because it is modest and domestic, it is nice evidence of the way a relatively inexpensive, mass-produced Book of Hours functioned c. 1520 – and especially so on the opening reproduced here. First, the picture – a damsel sitting on a stool, playing a lute, set inside a roundel inside a square with a background of acanthus leaves – has nothing devotional about it: it looks like a stereotypical lay image borrowed from stock. Was it, perhaps, designed to appeal to the female readers who, by 1520, were certainly buying Books of Hours in significant numbers? Second, the prayer that Germain Hardouyn has had printed above the image (which will be familiar to most English-speaking readers as 'God be in my head, and in my understanding') is in French. This is significant because, again, it suggests a particular market – one receptive to, and literate in, French, which might be attracted by a French-language prayer on the title-page. Third, on the left-hand leaf, some sixteenth-century owner has carefully copied out 'Veni Creator Spiritus', a Latin prayer dating from the ninth century which was felt to be particularly potent if recited at Pentecost: the reader has in effect personalised his volume. This is, in other words, very much a working private prayer-book.

Jane Taylor

donec proximus
Ductore sub te previo
vitemus omne noxium
Per te sciamus da
patrem noscamus
atque filium te utri
usque spiritum
credamus omni tempore
Sit laus patri cum
filio sancto simul
paraclito nobis que
mittat filius charis
ma sancti spiritus
amen amen AMEN

Jesus soit en ma teste et en mon entendement.
Jesus soit en mes yeulx et en mon regardement.
Jesus soit en ma bouche et en mon parlement.
Jesus soit en mon cueur et en mon pensement.
Jesus soit en ma vie et en mon trespassement.

Les presentes heures longues sont a lusaige de Romme toutes au long sans riens requerir ont este nouuellemēt Imprimees a Paris pour Germain Hardouyn libraire demourant au dict lieu entre les deulx portes du pallays a lenseigne saincte Marguerite et ce vendent au dict lieu.

THOMAS MORE VERSUS MARTIN LUTHER

27

Eruditissimi viri Ferdinandi Barauelli* [pseud., i.e. Thomas More] *opus ... quo retegit, ac refellit insanas Lutheri calumnias, quibus regem Henricum ... scurra turpissimus insectatur: excusum denuo diligentissime ...

[London:] 1523.

[362]p. 4°. 230 x 160 mm. STC 18088.5.

Provenance: Richard Sparchford (d. 1560); Laurentius Bruer; Martin Routh (Routh 14.B.17).

SB 0474

This is the only known copy of the first version of Thomas More's book against Martin Luther. In 1520 the latter published a major attack on the Roman Church, *De Babylonica Captivitate Ecclesiae*. In reply, King Henry VIII produced his *Assertio Septem Sacramentorum*, printed by Richard Pynson in London in 1521 and presented in Rome to Pope Leo X, who conferred on the author the title 'Fidei Defensor' which English monarchs have clung to ever since. More was one of the advisers who had helped the king in the work and indeed later claimed that he had then suggested that Henry might place rather less stress on papal authority.

In late 1522 Luther produced a virulent response to Henry's work and early in 1523 More set about a riposte in the same vein. This was printed, like the king's book, by Richard Pynson, but at first unacknowledged and represented as a reprint of a foreign edition, for on the title-page and in the prefatory pages its authorship is attributed to Ferdinandus Baravellus, a student in Spain. This version may have been sent to a few friends, such as Erasmus, by July 1523, but its distribution in that form must have been halted – by the king or More – in order to add much additional matter, utilising the original printed sheets as far possible and changing the preliminaries to a different fictional framework for another pseudonym, Gulielmus Rosseus, an Englishman in Italy, with a disclosure of its printing in England. Until the discovery of our copy of the first version, the bibliographical anomalies of the second, known from many copies, had had no attention, nor the full significance of the passages added in the expansion.

It appears by comparison that More now enlarged his point-by-point defence of Henry and the sacraments with a broader discussion of the nature of the Church, probably as a result of reading further controversy of Luther with other opponents. It must have been in the second half of 1523 that, after serving as Speaker of the House of Commons, he and Pynson altered the text substantially to the form of Rosseus, in which More also defends more fully the authority of the papacy – for which he died in 1535.

The woodcut border of the title-pages of both versions is of an unrelated Holbeinesque character, like others used by Pynson. Our copy of Baravellus may have been given to Cuthbert Tunstall, then Bishop of London, one of More's closest friends, for it bears an ownership inscription of Richard Sparchford (d. 1560), one of Tunstall's chaplains there. It is in a repaired blind-stamped binding with standard Tudor panels of John Raynes, a contemporary London stationer. It has a later inscription of Laurentius Bruer as purchaser, possibly one who matriculated from St John's College, Oxford, in 1629.

A. I. Doyle

ERVDITISSIMI VIRI
Ferdinādi Barauelli opus elegās, do-
ctum, festiuum, pium, quo pulcher-
rime retegit, ac refellit insanas Lutheri calumnias: quibus inuictissimum
Anglię, Galliæq; regem HENRI-
CVM eius nominis octauum, Fidei
defensorem, haud literis minus q̄ re-
gno clarum, scurra turpissimas insectatur: excusum denuo diligentissime, digestumq; in capita, ad-
iunctis indicibus opera
uiri doctissimi Io-
annis Car-
cellij.

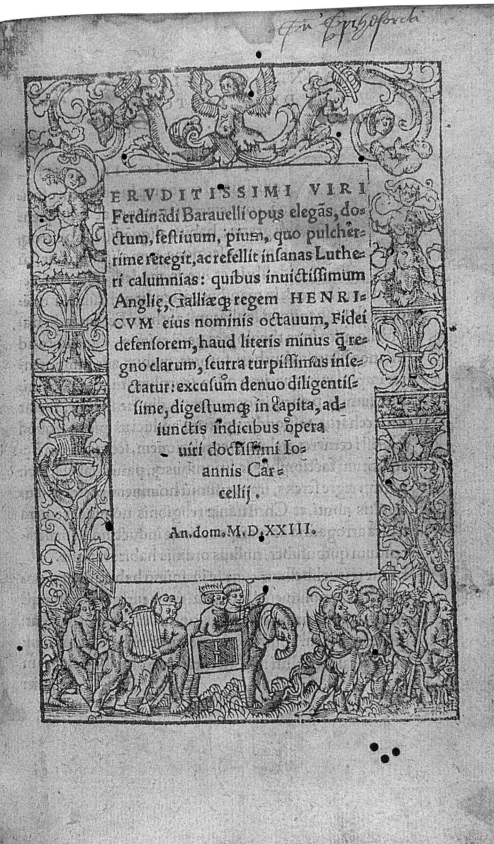

An. dom. M.D.XXIII.

RECYCLING MEDIEVAL MANUSCRIPTS

28

Antiphonal fragment: parchment manuscript written in ?Germany in the 15th century.

Single sheet 154 x 228 mm.

Provenance: Christian Suering, Basle, 1560; from the library of Martin Routh (Routh 14.I2.39).

SB 0366

Logica fragment: parchment manuscript written probably in northern France, Flanders or the Meuse region in the early 12th century.

Single sheet 208 x 168 mm.

Provenance: from the library of Maffeo Pinelli (d. 1785); acquired by Martin Routh (Routh 74.C.1).

SB 0360

One consequence of the religious upheavals of the sixteenth century was that many monastic library books and, above all, Latin service-books disappeared. As the new tide of protestantism ebbed and flowed across Europe, so the Latin services were replaced by simplified vernacular forms. In England, these in their turn were temporarily overthrown and the old order restored, then once more replaced by new forms of worship. The books used in these services were similarly banned and destroyed, suddenly rehabilitated, then finally thrown out once more. As monastic houses were suppressed, their libraries were scattered; if not salvaged by collectors or catholics, such volumes could become scrap. Huge quantities of parchment were re-used for anything from cloth-stiffening to organ building, from lamp-shades to pie-cases. Leaves were commonly used to wrap documents or were recycled in bindings of new books. Thus while the survival of complete medieval service-books is relatively rare in protestant countries and the contents of many medieval libraries have all but disappeared, nevertheless isolated leaves of such works are not uncommon, re-used in bindings as pastedowns, fly-leaves, hinges, or even actually forming the covers.

Both the 'host' books shown here were printed in Germany in the sixteenth century. The first contains two works: Thomas Cranmer's *A defence of the true and catholike doctrine of the sacrament* ... (Emden, 1557), bound with an edition of Paschasius' *De Spiritu sancto* (Cologne, 1539). The cover – a particularly fine example of the genre – has been formed from a leaf of a fifteenth century antiphonal, probably also from Germany. Paper pastedowns obscure the original text on the inside, but on the outside it is quite clear, blemished only by nineteenth-century shelf-mark labels on the spine and some darkening from exposure to the atmosphere. The service book would have been used in the choir for singing the continuous round of Latin services. The portion of the folio surviving here comprises part of a hymn for the octave of St Stephen, with the chant notation clearly marked on the four-line staff. It is well written in a bold hand, with a large red initial, to enable several people, gathered around a lectern, to use the antiphonal simultaneously. The words and notes are generally appropriately aligned, and the hymn could still be sung today.

The second book – Johann Fichard's *Vitae virorum* ...(biographies whose subjects include Petrarch, Colet and More), printed in Frankfurt in 1536 – has a limp, brown calf cover with a flap, the whole handsomely stamped with a repeating sequence of images, comprising the Fall of Man (labelled 'Peccatum'), the Brazen Serpent ('Signum fidei'), the Crucifixion ('Satisfactio'), and the Resurrection ('Justificatio'), a type of iconography embraced by early protestantism. Strengthening the cover within are recycled parts of folios of a Logica text dating from the earlier twelfth century. The work of two hands, one of north-eastern French or Mosan type, the other of northern French or English type, they are as clear and easy to read today as the later printed text they now protect.

M. M. N. Stansfield

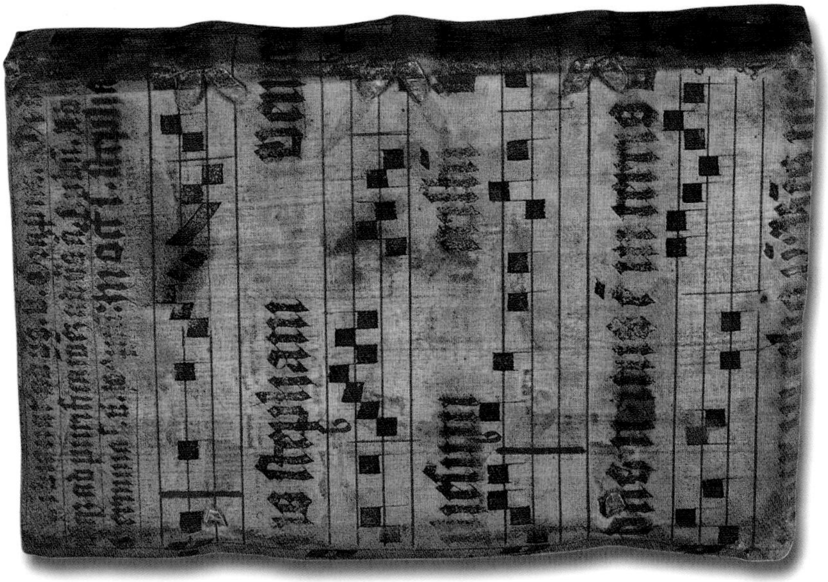

A Saffron 'Great Bible'

29

The Byble in Englyshe of the largest and greatest volume.

[London]: Richard Grafton, 1541.

[1], lxii, cviii, xcii, [2] leaves. 2º. 348 x 237 mm. Lacks Cranmer's prologue. STC 2073. DMH 63.

Provenance: inscription of Thomas Blackerby 1645; from Cosin's Library (Cosin A.1.10).

SB++ 0018

The 'Great Bible', so called because of its size, was effectively commissioned by Thomas Cromwell (*c.* 1485–1540) and Thomas Cranmer, archbishop of Canterbury (1489–1556), the two leading reformers under Henry VIII. In 1536, as Vicegerent-in-Spirituals, Cromwell had ordered all parishes to acquire a copy of the vernacular Bible. Though the 'Coverdale' Bible had been available from 1535, it did not command full support because it was not based on Hebrew and Greek texts. Therefore Cromwell appointed Miles Coverdale to provide a new translation: the 'Great Bible'. The first edition was printed in Paris, under Richard Grafton's supervision, by François Regnault because the English printing trade was insufficiently developed, technically and in terms of size, to cope with producing large complex books in significant numbers. But, after Regnault was reported for printing allegedly heterodox works, Grafton was forced to move the operation to London and cope as best he could. The 'Great Bible' was expensive, costing about £1 5s. It was perhaps fortunate, considering that 2500 copies may have been seized in Paris, that few of the 9000 parishes in England and Wales rushed to fulfil Cromwell's orders and purchase a copy in 1539. A royal injunction in May 1541 forced them to conform, with fines of forty shillings for every month's delay after 1 November. The numbers of Bibles, including the 'Great Bible', printed across the sixteenth century suggests there was also a demand from individuals. Unfortunately, we know nothing of the original owner of the present copy, or of the Thomas Blackerby who owned it in 1645, nor even how it entered Cosin's library.

This is the fourth edition, nominally revised by Cuthbert Tunstall (1474–1559), the conservative bishop of Durham, and Nicholas Heath (1501?–78), bishop of Rochester, one of Cranmer's allies. It was printed in 1541, after the execution of Cromwell, hence his arms were cut from the woodblock, leaving a blank circle to the right of the compartment. The Durham copy is notable for the yellow colour of its pages, seemingly the result of dyeing with saffron. A few Bibles and New Testaments (including another 1541 Great Bible), produced between 1536 and 1579, exhibit the same characteristic. While its precise significance is unclear, it assimilates these paper books to parchment ones, enhancing their venerability.

The 'Great Bible' not only played an important role in the establishment of Protestantism, but helped to form an iconographic tradition for the English Reformation. Its title page depicts Henry VIII, in the guise of David, handing copies of the vernacular Bible (paradoxically labelled *Verbum dei*) to members of the clergy and laity led by Cranmer and Cromwell. The two reformers then disseminate the text to kneeling clerics, deferential magistrates and obedient subjects, including prisoners (bottom right corner), all of whom intone 'Vivat Rex' and 'God save the King'. This powerful image has traditionally been seen as an example of Tudor royal propaganda, broadcasting the crown's role in establishing the new faith. However, recent research has demonstrated that the image was actually part of a concerted campaign by Cranmer and Cromwell to encourage Henry to take on this role. A crucial piece of internal evidence is the relative conservatism of the image. First, Henry does not exhort his clergy and laity to evangelise as the reformers wanted; instead he emphasises reverence for and submission to, divine authority: 'I make a decree that in all the dominion of my kingdom, men tremble and feare before the God of Daniel: for he is the living God' (Daniel 6.26). Second, the common people receive the word of God from a preacher and are exhorted to pray for the king rather than to proselytise or discuss scripture.

Natalie Mears

The Byble in
Englyshe of the largest and grea-
by the commaundement of oure moost
Kynge Henrye the. viii. supreme head
Englande: to be frequented and
sayd realme, accordynge to the
tuccions geuen in
that behalfe.
maundemet of the kynges hyghnes,
Cuthbert byshop of Duresme, and Ni-
colas bisshop of Rochester.
Cum priuilegio ad imprimendum solum.
1541.
VIVAT REX
GOD SAVE THE KINGE

An Embroidered Presentation Binding

30

Francis Bacon, *The essayes or counsels, ciuill and morall … Newly enlarged.*

London: printed by Iohn Havilland for Hanna Barret, and Richard Whittaker, 1625.

[10], 340p. 4°. 215 x 160 mm. STC 1148.

Provenance: possibly presented by the author to Charles I, by whom perhaps given to John Cosin (Cosin Y.4.6).

SB 2396

This copy of the *Essayes* of Francis Bacon (1561–1626) has a splendid binding of green velvet embroidered with silver thread and purl and with spangles scattered through the pattern. In the centre of each cover is a portrait of George Villiers, first Duke of Buckingham, done in coloured silks on white satin, within a frame of silver thread. Although slightly different in size and in features, the portraits are obviously taken from a single source – an engraving by Simon de Passe (*c.* 1595–1647). Their detail is very fine, with tiny buttons down the front of the doublet, a pearl earring in one ear, and carefully-drawn features. Above the frame of each picture was a royal crown done in red silk and silver purl; that on the front cover has been removed. The spine has seven compartments with stylised flowers in silver thread, and there are the remains of red silk ties. The edges of the leaves are gilt.

An almost identical, though better preserved, binding is now at the Bodleian Library, to which it was given in November 1628 by a London merchant. The embroidered design is the same as the Cosin copy and once again there are two slightly different versions of the portrait in mirror image; however, instead of a royal crown above Buckingham's head, there is a ducal coronet on each cover.

The mid-sixteenth to the mid-seventeenth century was a golden age for English embroidery. Embroidered textiles decorated houses and were used luxuriantly in clothing, and it is no surprise that when a presentation copy of a printed book was needed, the portrait binding was used as the equivalent of the illuminated presentation page in a medieval manuscript. The high quality embroidered bindings were created by professionals, but not much is known of their organisation and methods. Owing to the fragility of the textiles used – velvet, silk and linen – well-preserved examples are comparatively rare.

Sir Francis Bacon's *Essayes*, the work contained in this binding, was entered in the Stationers' Register on 13 March 1625 and was dedicated to the Duke of Buckingham, his longstanding friend and patron. In this third enlarged edition, published the year before the author's death, the themes of friendship and royal patronage are more fully explored. By the time of Buckingham's assassination in 1628, John Cosin was also indebted to the duke for the king's preferment of the living of Brancepeth.

The two presentation copies of Bacon's *Essayes* in their ornate silver and velvet bindings were probably commissioned by the author as gifts to the dedicatee, Buckingham (the Bodleian copy with its ducal coronets), and either James I or more probably Charles, Prince of Wales (the Durham copy with its royal crowns). It is quite conceivable that Charles could have given his copy to Cosin, an admirer of Buckingham, and a loyal royalist. When and why the royal crown was ripped from the front cover are open questions.

Sheila Hingley

John Cosin's French Library

31

Isabeau Bernard de Lagnes, ***Remonstrances aux parlementaires d'Angleterre, sur la mort ignominieuse de leur Roy.***

Paris: N. Charles, [1649].

[8], 29, [1]p. 8°. 190 x 120 mm.

Provenance: probably presented by the author to Queen Henrietta Maria and given by her to John Cosin.

Cosin W.5.2

John Cosin's episcopal library comprises, in effect, three consecutive collections: his acquisitions in Cambridge and Durham before the Civil War; the library he formed in exile in France, 1644–60; then the substantial additions he made when bishop of Durham, 1660–72.

Among the treasures acquired during the middle period are the works of a fellow-exile, Thomas Hobbes, to whom, when he was gravely ill in 1646, Cosin ministered. Cosin's Library has a large paper copy of the genuine first edition of *Leviathan* (London, 1651: Hobbes corrected the proofs in Paris), and also the rare variant of the second edition of *De Cive* (Amsterdam, 1647), with pencil marks by Cosin in the margins where Hobbes says that only a few copies have been printed for friends.

The collection of books in French is no less remarkable in itself. Cosin's French library is the finest of its kind and period in Britain. There are 585 items in French, many of extreme rarity. Of the works with known authors, no fewer than eighty are not represented in any edition in the Bibliothèque nationale de France, Paris, while at least a further seventy are in editions not held there; and to these one can add a very substantial number of anonymous works.

The collection is typically personal and distinctive. Always a man of warm and responsive humanity, Cosin was appalled by the arrogant and predatory unpleasantness of the Roman Catholic theologians whom he encountered in Paris, and – astonishingly for this eminent Laudian Arminian – increasingly attracted by the kindness and generosity of the Protestants. This gives his French library a completely different character from his earlier collection.

Four hundred of the works are religious books and pamphlets, 305 of them by French Reformed or other Calvinist authors, the overwhelming majority of whom were contemporaries of Cosin. About a hundred different French Protestant writers are represented, with exceptionally valuable holdings of ten of the most important of them, including Pierre Du Moulin (1568–1658), the outstanding Huguenot writer of the century, Charles Drelincourt, Jean Mestrezat, Jean Daillé, David Blondel and Moïse Amyraut. Cosin had a particular taste for their sermons, of which more than 500 appear in his collection.

There is also an extremely interesting group of works giving the French perspective on the English troubles. The work illustrated is the unique surviving copy of a long poem of 1649, written by a lady, Dame Isabeau Bernard de Lagnes, protesting at the execution of Charles I. Dame Isabeau, who had already published a collection of devotional verse, is hopelessly ill-informed on Protestant theology (she fiercely attacks Cromwell's Lutheranism), but compensates with her passionate moral fury and unstoppable rhetorical indignation. The work is dedicated to the widowed Queen Henrietta Maria, who, presumably not knowing what else to do with it, must have passed it on to Cosin, the Anglican chaplain of her household. Engaging in its oddity, it is characteristic of the unexpected discoveries to be made in all the Durham special collections.

Richard Maber

REMONSTRANCES AVX PARLEMENTAIRES D'ANGLETERRE, SVR LA MORT IGNOMINIEVSE de leur Roy.

DEDIE'ES
A la Royne d'Angleterre.

Compoſées par Dame Iſabeau Bernard de Lagnes, vefue de feu Monſieur de Saluancy, Mere de la Congregation du Tiers Ordre ſacré du glorieux Pere S. Dominique.

A PARIS,
Chez N. CHARLES, aux trois Couronnes, proche de ſainct Hilaire, au College de la Mercy.

Auec Permiſsion.

GRAND MEDITATIONS ON LIFE AND DEATH 32

Thomas Browne, *Hydriotaphia, urne-buriall, or, a discourse of the sepulchrall urnes lately found in Norfolk.*

London: printed for Henry Brome, 1658.

[16], 102 [i.e. 202], [6] p. 8°. 165 x 115 mm. Wing B 5154.

Provenance: presented by the author to John Robins; 17th/18th-century owners include William Harmer and T. Barber of Norfolk (armorial bookplate); from the collection of Bishop Edward Maltby.

SB 0027

On his retirement from the see of Durham in 1856, Bishop Edward Maltby (1770–1859) left his library to the University. The collection consists of around 1500 titles, and is particularly strong in classical, theological and philological texts. It also contains some important works of science and literature, of which this rare author-annotated first edition of *Hydriotaphia* is of exceptional interest.

Sir Thomas Browne (1605–82) is an important figure in early modern science, religion and literature, a natural philosopher, and one of the finest and most original early modern English stylists, who substantially broadened the English language with his coinages.

Hydriotaphia is Browne's great meditation on death and immortality, prompted by the discovery of a hoard of grave urns in a field at Old Walsingham, Norfolk. Browne considers the history of burial and cremation rites, then discusses the Walsingham urns themselves, speculating on their origins; he moves increasingly from the factual into the realm of the transcendental, considering the theological motives behind funerary practices, culminating in the final book's rhapsody on the vanity of human monuments in the face of the imminent demise of the earth. Whilst the tone these 'sad and sepulchral Pitchers' inspire is often bleak, *Hydriotaphia* is ultimately a celebration of the Christian view of mortality with its promise of resurrection.

The Garden of Cyrus was published in the same volume; if *Hydriotaphia* is Browne's great investigation of death, *Cyrus* is his great study of the forms of life. Browne's ostensible subject is quincunxes, figures of five, which he traces in both the natural and man-made worlds, and which he discovers to be millenarian signatures of divine cultivation, and the promise of renewal. But *Cyrus* is also about the spontaneous nature of germination – the most important discovery of early-modern biology. Browne's scientific rigour is demonstrated in his attention to the structure of the flora of his native East Anglia; and his study of procreation ranges from seeds through to insects and the higher animals. Ultimately Browne integrates generation as a metaphor for divine purpose: 'the verdant state of things is the symbol of the Resurrection, and to flourish in the state of glory we must first be sown in corruption'.

In the present copy, inscribed by Browne to his 'worthy and honourd friend Mr John Robins', the author has inserted some forty-two corrections, six of which are independent of the *errata* of both first and second editions. Typography was of particular importance to Browne, a man preoccupied by the restitutive correction of error, and whose first work, *Religio Medici*, had been pre-emptively and carelessly published in an opportunistic pirated edition. The practical effect of his concern can be seen here in the meticulous care with which he has perfected the text of this copy before presenting it to his friend.

Peter Maber

HYDRIOTAPHIA,

URNE-BURIALL,

OR,

A Diſcourſe of the Sepulchrall Urnes lately found in *NORFOLK.*

Together with

The Garden of *CYRUS,*

OR THE

Quincunciall, Lozenge, or Net-work Plantations of the Ancients, Artificially, Naturally, Myſtically Conſidered.

With Sundry Obſervations.

By *Thomas Browne* D. of Phyſick.

LONDON,

Printed for *Hen. Brome* at the Signe of the Gun in *Ivy-lane.* 1658.

33

The Durham Book

The booke of common prayer and administration of the sacraments.

London: Robert Barker and John Bill, 1619.

Annotated in 1626–7 and 1660–1 by John Cosin, bishop of Durham, and by his chaplain, William Sancroft. 2 pts in 1v. ([300]; [160] p.). 2°. 355 x 235 mm. STC 16353.

Provenance: John Cosin.

Cosin D.3.5

The 'Durham Book' has a celebrated role in the history of the Church of England. It is a 1619 folio edition of the *Book of Common Prayer* that was subsequently carefully annotated in preparation for the revision of the Prayer Book after the restoration of the monarchy in 1660.

Thomas Cranmer's second Prayer Book of 1552 had embodied a clearly protestant understanding of worship appropriate to the Church of England's character as a reformed church. That book was a thoroughgoing revision of his first Prayer Book of 1549. However, it had satisfied neither the puritan party for whom it was not radical enough, nor the emerging 'high church' group associated with Archbishop William Laud (1573–1645) who sought to emphasise in the liturgy the church's debt to its catholic past. Among its leaders was John Cosin (1594–1672), bishop of Durham.

Cosin began to annotate his copy of the Prayer Book as early as 1626–7 when he was a canon of Durham Cathedral and rector of Brancepeth. During this time he devoted much energy to elaborating the ceremonial of the Cathedral, not without controversy. Most annotations in the 'Durham Book', however, belong to the period 1660–61 following his return from exile during the Commonwealth. They are written in the clear italic hand of a renaissance man, often squeezed into tiny spaces on the page and with numerous scribbles and crossings–out; yet they remain legible today. They are in the spirit of his earlier Durham period (though time had moderated his more extreme opinions) and draw on sources such as Cranmer's 1549 Prayer Book and the much admired Scottish rite of 1637, for Laudians a benchmark of liturgical excellence. (Some annotations are the work of William Sancroft, the Bishop's chaplain and later Archbishop of Canterbury.)

Cosin was as much concerned with rubrics governing the performance of the liturgy as with the spoken words themselves. He looked for Anglican ceremonial that was ordered and dignified, 'catholic' but not sacrificing what properly belonged to a church of the Reformation. In this, he found the 1552 book not only theologically deficient but lacking in clarity and consistency. For example, at the Prayer of Consecration in the Communion rite (illustrated overleaf), Cosin adds rubrics, absent in 1552, directing the priest to perform actions imitating those of the Last Supper: to take the paten, to break the bread, and to lay hands over it. These instructions were to find their way into the definitive text of the 1662 *Book of Common Prayer*. However, many of his ideas were not accepted, no doubt because of his 'advanced' views in a volatile age when forms of public worship would always be a delicately negotiated (and hard-won) compromise.

The treasure of Cosin's library is of a piece with his dignified furnishings in Durham Cathedral across the green. They both speak of the spirituality, sobriety, proportion and debt to a cherished Christian tradition that lay at the heart of his beliefs about the Church of England, expressed so eloquently in the book of 1662 one of whose principal architects he can truly be said to have been.

Michael Sadgrove

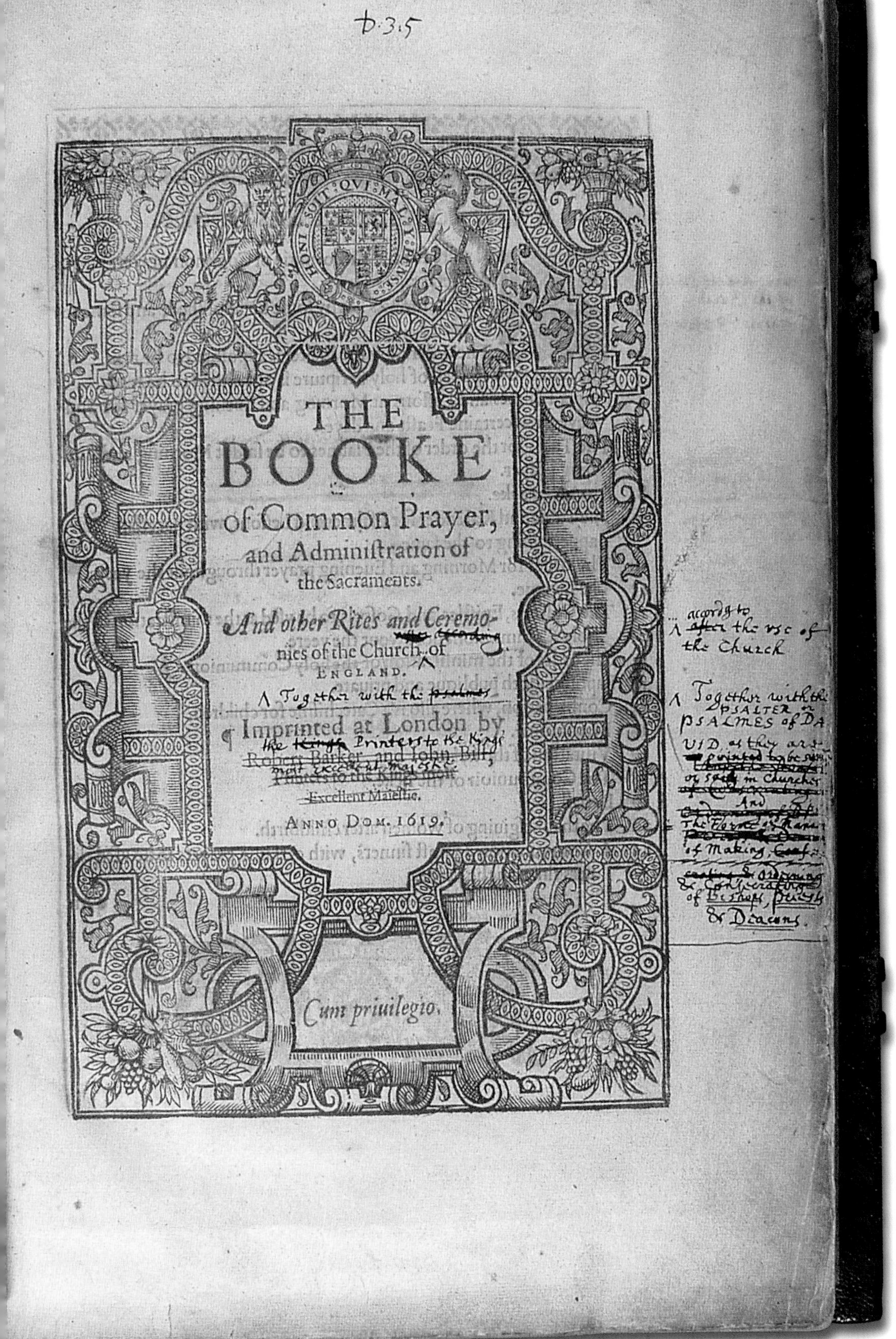

D.3.5

THE BOOKE

of Common Prayer, and Administration of the Sacraments.

And other Rites and Ceremonies of the Church ~~[illegible] ~~according~~~~ of ENGLAND.

Together with the ~~psalmes~~

¶ Imprinted at London by the ~~Kings~~ Printers to the Kings ~~Robert Barker and John Bill,~~ most excellent maiestie ~~Printers to the Kings most Excellent Maiestie.~~

ANNO DOM. 1619.

Cum priuilegio.

according to ~~after~~ the vse of the Church

Together with the PSALTER or PSALMES of DAVID as they are ~~pointed to be sung~~ or said in Churches

And

The Forme & Maner of Making, ~~Conse-~~ ~~crating~~ & ordaining & Consecrating of Bishops, Priests & Deacons.

uent zeale, constantly to preach the Gospel unto all nations: whereby we ~~are~~ brought out of darkenesse and errour, into the cleare light and true knowledge of thee, and of thy Sonne Jesus Christ. Therefore with Angels, &c.

^ have bin

Upon the Feast of Trinitie ~~onely~~.

IT is very meete, right, and our bounden duetie, that wee should at all times & in all places giue thankes to thee, O Lord, Almighty and euerlasting God, ~~which~~ art one God, one Lord, not one onely person, but three persons in one substance. For that which we beleeue of the glory of the Father the same wee beleeue of the Sonne, and of the holy Ghost, without any difference, or inequalitie. Therefore, &c.

Begin ye Proper Preface here

~~divine~~

After which Prefaces, shall ~~follow~~ immediatly ~~shall~~ be sung or said

THerefore with Angels and Archangels, and with all the company of heauen, wee laude and magnifie thy glorious Name, euermore praising thee, and saying, Holy, holy, holy, Lord God of hostes, Heauen and earth are full of thy glory. Glory be to thee, O Lord most high. Amen.

Here followeth the Prayer of Consecration

When the priest standing before ye Table hath so ordered the Bread & Wine ~~placed upon the Table~~ that he may with the more readiness & decency break the Bread before the people & take the Cup into his hands ~~standing up~~ he shall say, as followeth. Almighty God &c as in ye next page.

Then shall the Priest kneeling downe at Gods Board, say in the name of all them that shall receiue the Communion, this prayer following.

WEe doe not presume to come to this thy Table (O mercifull Lord) trusting in our owne righteousnesse, but in thy manifold and great mercies. Wee be not worthy so much as to gather up the crumbes under thy Table. But thou art the same Lord, whose propertie is alwayes to haue mercy: graunt us therefore gracious Lord, so to eate the flesh of thy deare Sonne Jesus Christ, and to drinke his blood, that our sinnefull bodies may be made cleane by his body, and our soules washed thorow his most precious blood, and that wee may euermore dwell in him, and he in us. Amen.

~~in these holy Mysteries~~

Then

Then shall the priest that celebrateth ~~first~~ receive the holy Communion in both kinds himselfe ~~and~~ ~~deliver the same to the Bishops, priests, & Deacons (if any be present)~~ & after to the people in due order, into their hands, all humbly kneeling: ~~And when he delivereth the Body of Christ~~ he delivereth ~~the Body of Christ to any one~~ he shall say

The Body of our Lord &c, as in ye next page.

Then shall he stand up & proceed to deliver the holy Communion first to the Bishops, priests, & Deacons (if any be present) in both kinds, & after &c.

And when he taketh the Sacrament of ye Body of Christ he shall say

The Body of our Lord Jesus Christ which was given for mee, preserve my Body & Soule unto everlasting life. Amen. I take & eate this in remembrance that Christ dyed for me, & I feed on Him in my heart by faith with thanksgiving.

And when he taketh ye Sacrament of Christs Blood, he shall say,

The Blood of our Lord &c

so continue as is most meet at the delivery of ye Whole Comunion

The Prayer of Consecration

~~Then the Priest standing vp, shall say as followeth.~~

ALmighty God, our heauenly Father, which of thy tender mercy diddest giue thy onely Sonne Jesus Christ to suffer death vpon the Crosse for our redemption, who made there (by his one oblation of himselfe once offered) a full, perfect, and sufficient sacrifice, oblation, and satisfaction for the sins of the whole world, and did institute, and in his holy Gospel command vs to continue a perpetuall memory of that his precious death, vntill his comming againe: Heare vs, O mercifull Father, we beseech thee, and ~~grant that we, receiuing these thy creatures of Bread and Wine,~~ according to thy Sonne our Sauiour Jesus Christs holy institution, in remembrance of his death and passion, may be partakers of his most blessed Body and Blood: who in the same night that hee was betrayed, tooke Bread, and when he had giuen thankes he brake it, and gaue it to his disciples, saying, Take, eat, this is my Body which is giuen for you, doe this in remembrance of mee. Likewise after Supper he tooke the Cup, and when hee had giuen thankes he gaue it to them, saying, Drinke ye all of this, for this is my Blood of the new Testament, which is shed for you and for many for the remission of sinnes: doe this as oft as ye shall drinke it, in remembrance of me. Amen

Immediately after shall follow the Memoriall or prayer of Oblation.
Wherfore O Lord &c, as in ye next page

~~Then shal the Minister first receiue the Communion in both kinds himselfe, and next deliuer it to other Ministers (if any be there present) that they may helpe the chiefe Minister, and after, to the people in their hands, kneeling. And when he deliuereth the Bread, he shal say,~~

THe Body of our Lord Jesus Christ, which was giuen for thee, preserue thy body and soule into euerlasting life: ~~and~~ take and eate this in remembrance ~~that~~ Christ dyed for thee, and feed on him in thine heart by faith, with thankesgiuing.

And

And here each person receiving shall say [Amen.] Then shall the priest adde, Take & Eate &c.

~~celebrate &~~
& Sacrifice
most humbly
~~vouchsafe~~ by ye power of thy holy word & Spirit vouchsafe so to blesse & sanctifie these thy gifts & Creatures of Bread & wine, that wee receiving them
Him, & to shew forth
~~blessed &~~
~~blessed &~~

At these words [took: Bread] the priest is to take y^e^ paten into his Hands, at [brake it] to break the Bread, & at [This is my Body] to lay his hand upon it.
= At these words [took the Cup] the priest is to take the chalice into his hands, & at [This is my Blowd] to lay his hand upon every vessel (be it Chalice or flagon) in wch there is wine to be consecrated.
If any Bread or wine be wanting, the priest is to consecrate more, as is before appointed, beginning with [Our Saviour Christ in ye same night &c] for ye blessing of the Bread; & at [Likewise after Supper &c] for the blessing of the Cup.

omit this here & set it y^e^ [illegible]

[illegible] ye BB at [illegible] ordered all in ye old Method, thus. First ye prayer of Address. We do not presume &c. then ye Rubrick, then ye priest standing &c. ye prayer of Consecration unaltered (only one for our. & Amen at last) with ye marginal Rubrics. Then (ye Memorial or prayer of oblation omitted, & ye L^ds^ prayer) follow ye Rubricks & Forms of Participation, & Distribution to ye end of ye Rubrick. When all have [illegible] &c. altogether as in this book; only ye Rubrick for ye Coion time shall be sung &c. wth ye Sentences following wholly omitted. And y^n^ ye Lords prayer, & Collect O L^d^, & Hear. F. &c. &c to ye end

A Seventeenth-Century Emblem-Book 34

Otto van Veen, *Quinti Horatii Flacci Emblemata, imaginibus in aes incisis, notisque illustrata.*

Brussels: Franciscus Foppens, 1683.

[8], 205, [3] p. 4°. 285 x 235 mm.

Provenance: from the collection of the Edleston family of Gainford.

SB+ 0123

The Library holds many early modern illustrated books that explore the relationship between text and image. Techniques of printed book production, coupled with the sophistication of copper-plate engraving, made for attractive and marketable volumes in which words and pictures 'talked' to each other. Nowhere were text and image more intriguingly juxtaposed than in the emblem-book. A typical emblem-book headed pages with a gnomic 'motto' that encapsulated the meaning of the image. The image itself assembled realistically-depicted objects, animals, and human figures in an enigmatic composition that demanded interpretation. Words printed below the image or on the facing page responded with an explanation, usually conveying a moral message. Our *Emblemata* from the Roman poet Horace (d. 8 BC), with its 103 engravings, reproduces pictures designed by Otto van Veen (1556–1629), a painter who taught Rubens. It was first printed in 1607, but the library's 1683 edition belongs to the period when it was most popular. Additions and changes to this edition emphasise elements that made it much more than an emblem-book. The upper section of each verso assembles Latin quotations all related to the sense of the lines from Horace, which from the first edition were clearly the genesis of the picture opposite. These collected excerpts make this a commonplace-book, the most useful tool for any Renaissance writer wanting to amplify a topic with choice sentiments in good Latin. The arrangement of the book as a whole also replicates commonplace-books ordered under topics linked by affinity and opposition. The original prose elucidation of the picture is swamped by these quotations, or omitted altogether. In the lower half of the verso and below the picture opposite, are verses in Italian, Dutch and French (twice). The Italian and Dutch paraphrase Horace's lines with close attention to the picture. The French transpose them into the more vapid literary style of seventeenth-century France and accommodate them to its mores. This production is for the international market. The elegant pictures are remarkable for their realistic detail and for the ease with which they turn every hint of allegorical abstraction in Horace's lines into a coherent pictorial language of allegorical figures, with attributes derived from the more recondite sources of Cesare Ripa's *Iconologia*. Our book is for the intellectually curious as well as for picture-browsers. The 'motto' subsuming text and image in the pages reproduced here is: 'Excessive fear of poverty is bad for liberty'. The ragged, unkempt figure of Poverty to whom the subservient figure surrenders his cap of liberty is fully allegorised, with empty bag and bowl, carrot, and cabbage for attributes. The rich man rides the poor man like an ass, reins attached to his mouth. In the background, the poor man's lot is to be whipped to work like a horse in a mill, a barn goes up in smoke, and a man trundles his family away in a wheelbarrow. All this grows perceptibly, but graphically, out of the lines quoted from Horace. The Dutch and Italian verses clue us in more strongly. The French have completely lost the plot.

Ann Moss

NIMIUS PAUPERTATIS METUS LIBERTATI NOXIUS.

Lib. 1. Epist. 10.

Sic, qui pauperiem veritus, potiore metallis
Libertate caret, dominum vehet improbus, atque
Serviet æternùm, quia parvo nesciet uti.

Vides hunc miserum, propter nimium paupertatis metum, libertatis pileum abdicantem! Atque idem iste, cernis, ut dorso Asini instar herum auro onustum vehat? Quinimo ad pistrinum flagellis se cogi patiatur.

Menand. *Paupertatem ferre non omnis, sed viri sapientis.*

Juvenal. Sat. 3.

Libertas pauperis hæc est,
Pulsatus rogat, & pugnis concisus adorat,
Ut liceat paucis cum dentibus inde reverti.

Chi dal timor di Povertà commosso
La ricca libertà misero vende,
Del Ricco si fa servo, e porta al dosso
Fatto asino il signor, che d'oro splende,
Con la sforza del oro vien percosso,
E mille indignità soffre, & attende.
Libero, e ricco è l'huom contento; è servo
L'intemperato, e il poverel protervo.

Vrees voor armoe maakt slaaven.

Een, die door't vreezen voor gebrék
Zyn' vryheid veilt, is dubbel gék:
Hy dient wél eeuwig slaaf te weezen
Voor weinig goud, én in die staat
Der Ryken dwinglandy te vreezen,
En lyden overlast, én smaad.
De vryheid, waerdiger, dan't leeven,
Wordt dwaaslyk voor wat gelds gegeeven.

Riche infame, il est vray: Les Estoiles ingrates
T'ont fait tyran du pauvre, & t'ont mis sous ta loy.
Mais s'il est magnanime, il est plus grand que toy;
Et tel que fut Cesar au milieu des Pirates,
Bien qu'il soit ton esclave, il te commande en Roy.

LA

LA CRAINTE DE LA PAUVRETE' EST NUISIBLE A LA LIBERTE'.

Que d'effects malheureux fait dans une ame vile
Cette apprehension, cette crainte servile
Que plusieurs des humains ont de la pauvreté,
C'est elle qui leur fait commettre cent bassesses,
Et mesme quelquefois vendre leur Liberté,
Et faire bien souvent mille tours de souplesses.

SORS

HISTORIÆ CŒLESTIS
LIBRI PRIMI,
PARS TERTIA;
Cometarum & Planetarum Primariorum.
A Fixis DISTANTIAS
GRENOVICI
In Observatorio Regio,
Ab Anno 1676, ad Annum 1689.
SEXTANTE Captas,
COMPLECTENS.

OBSERVATIONES COMETÆ,
ANNI MDCLXXVII

Mapping the Heavens

35

John Flamsteed, *Historia coelestis Britannica.*

London: J. Matthews, 1712.

2 parts in 1 v. ([4], vi, 60; 360, 361–362 leaves, 363–387, [1]; [2], 120, [2] p.)
2°. 405 x 275 mm.

Provenance: gold cartouche of the Bignon library on binding; armorial bookplate of Thomas John Hussey of Hayes, Kent, who presented the book to the University in 1850.

SC+ 00043

John Flamsteed (1646–1719) was the First Astronomer Royal, having been appointed to head the new Greenwich Observatory by King Charles II in 1675. His task was to map the heavens and thereby devise a method for determining longitude at sea. Newton and Halley (who was eventually to be Flamsteed's successor at Greenwich) were keen to see the method succeed and Newton, in particular, leaned heavily on Flamsteed to publish his observations. Clearly, Newton wanted the data for his own, largely original, work on planetary orbits.

Flamsteed, however, was a perfectionist. As a sickly child and teenager he had been educated privately and had not had the advantage of a university education. Perhaps this accounted for his unwillingness to publish before he had checked and checked again. Nevertheless, Newton, as President of The Royal Society (1703–27) – and as effectively Chairman of the Governors of the Observatory – persevered, with the result that the present volume appeared. From the start, however, Flamsteed was dissatisfied and proceeded to recall the volumes. Nevertheless, some remained in circulation, of which the present volume is one. It is interesting to note that Spencer Cowper (1713–74), dean of Durham, a man interested in Meteorology and Astronomy, bequeathed a copy of the later, acceptable-to-Flamsteed, version of the book in question to the Dean and Chapter Library in Durham (H. VI. 13–15). Thus, the University Library has the original, 'illegal' copy of the book and the cathedral has the later approved copy; there is perhaps a profound message here!

Now to *Historia coelestis Brittanica* itself. It is a remarkable collection of stellar positions by constellation, given to the nearest second of arc, together with observations on comets and planets (Newton would have been happy). There are also data on lunar occultations. Each section is surmounted by an impressive engraving; that on page 103 is illustrated here. The Introduction mentions the 'astronomical greats': Tycho Brahe, Jonas Moore, Christopher Wren (an astronomer before he became an architect), Isaac Newton and Edmond Halley. There cannot be many other books of the period, in the scientific area at least, that have had such an interesting history.

As a footnote, it can be added that the eventual solution of the longitude problem came not from 'the astronomical method' but rather using horology – Harrison's superb watch, 'H4'. After much Government skullduggery (nothing changes), Harrison received the £20,000 offered by the 1714 Longitude Act. He, Harrison, is now 'memorialized' in Westminster Abbey, the ceremony being conducted by Prince Philip on 24 March 2006.

Arnold Wolfendale

The First Large-Scale Map of Co. Durham

36

The county palatine of Durham survey'd by Capt. Armstrong and engraved by Thomas Jefferys Geographer to his Majesty.

London: printed for R. Sayer and T. Jeffreys, Feb.15 1768.

Map in 4 sheets. Complete map: 940 x 1240 mm.

NSR Planfile C 19/3/1–4

In the later sixteenth century the first sets of printed English county maps appeared, associated with Christopher Saxton, John Speed, and the great Dutch atlas publishers. These were designed to fit an atlas opening, about 40 x 50 cm, and showed major features, such as towns and rivers, but lacked roads and other practical details. These maps were re-used, often reduced to fit smaller formats, for two centuries. By the mid-eighteenth century they were obviously outdated and, goaded by recent progress in France, the newly formed Society for the Encouragement of Arts, Manufactures and Commerce offered a prize of £100 for accurately surveyed 1-inch-to-the-mile county maps. While this would not have covered the cost of surveying and publishing such works, it would have been a useful financial contribution, and success would enhance the creator's reputation and lead to patronage. The bounty also enforced professional trigonometrical surveying standards, requiring use of a theodolite and a 'perambulator' to measure road distances.

Publishing maps had always been an expensive risk, requiring particular skills and equipment, and tended to be done by a small group of specialists. Thomas Jefferys was one of the main cartographic engravers of his generation, but managed to bankrupt himself in 1766 trying to produce county maps. This financial situation may explain why Armstrong's map appeared with three different imprints in 1768.

This first large-scale map of County Durham, the product of the new scientific method, is the earliest known published survey work of Andrew Armstrong (1700–94). Although this was not entered for the Society's prize, his 1769 map of Northumberland did win, and his entry gives rare information on the costs of producing maps at the time. The larger nine-sheet Northumberland map took him three years to survey, the cost to survey, engrave and print 500 copies being £516. 10s. The 1768 map of Durham was printed on four 21 x 27½ inch sheets, each plate 19½ x 25¼ inches. Most maps would be joined and mounted on cloth, and then discarded due to wear or obsolescence, so this copy is a rare example of how a newly-printed map would appear.

The detail (top quarter of the top-left sheet) shows the elaborate title vignette, which usually featured the regional economy – here the early coal trade and millstone quarrying. Armstrong has also underlined the new scientific standards to which his work adheres with a diagram of the triangulation upon which it is based (and elsewhere cites the authorities for his latitude and longitude). The depicted area of Weardale illustrates the use of hachures to represent relief, the rivers and some roads following the valleys, with a few isolated settlements. Larger houses are accompanied by the names of their owners – potential customers who would be wooed by these citations. Coal pits and lead mines are marked, and the different quality roads are distinguished. Armstrong's antiquarian interest is clear from his tracing of Roman remains, with an accurate map of Durham City added in the bottom left corner. A second edition was published in 1791, and Armstrong's remained the largest scale map of County Durham until the work of the Ordnance Survey in the 1850s.

Richard Higgins

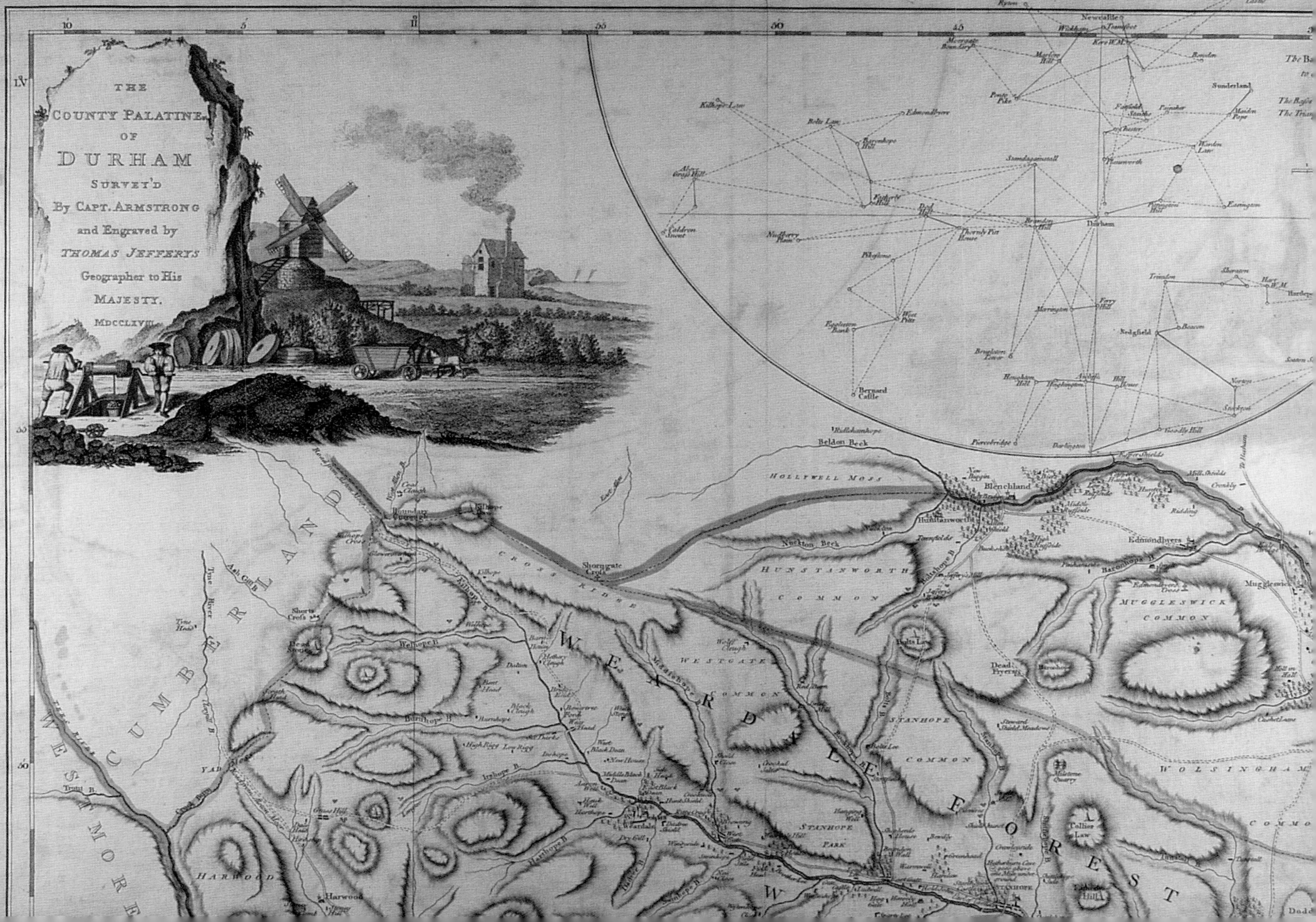
THE
COUNTY PALATINE
OF
DURHAM
SURVEY'D
By CAPT. ARMSTRONG
and Engraved by
THOMAS JEFFERYS
Geographer to His
MAJESTY.
MDCCLXVIII
Durham
Sunderland
Newcastle
Sedgfield
Darlington
Bernard Castle
Blenchland
Edmondbyers
HOLLYWELL MOSS
CROSS RIDGE
HUNSTANWORTH COMMON
MUGGLESWICK COMMON
WESTGATE COMMON
STANHOPE COMMON
STANHOPE PARK
WOLSINGHAM
WEARDALE
FOREST
CUMBERLAND
WESTMORE
Harwood

PLATE
IX.

A New Theory of the Earth

37

Thomas Wright of Durham, ***A New Theory of the Earth founded upon and more fully explaining the universal phenomenon of earthquakes; the magnet and doctrine of tides.***

Paper manuscript *c.* 1773. [125] loose leaves, XII plates. 220 x 170 mm.

Provenance: possibly from the library of Shute Barrington, bishop of Durham (d.1826); acquired in 2002.

Thomas Wright MS 18/1

Thomas Wright (1711–86) was born in Byers Green, Co. Durham, and received his primary education in Bishop Auckland, Gateshead and Sunderland. A self-taught polymath, he became a tutor to the aristocracy and a successful author of works on natural philosophy, mathematics, gardening and architecture. In 1742 he was offered a post at the Imperial Academy at St Petersburg (which he declined), and in 1750 he published his most popular book, *An Original Theory of the Universe*, which is primarily remembered for its description of the Milky Way and for the impact that its ideas had upon the philosopher Immanuel Kant. Over the course of his career he produced hundreds of pages of letters, notes and drawings; many of which were turned into pamphlets, paper tools, engraved diagrams, study guides and wall-charts.

A New Theory of the Earth is a manuscript book written around 1773. Its intellectual foundation is the canon of texts employed by humanists across Europe during the early modern period and the Enlightenment. First taught in households, parish schools and academies, then in universities, this canon included the Bible along with various classical, patristic and Renaissance works and incorporated a select group of new books associated with the Scientific Revolution. It allowed Wright to cite Copernicus, Kepler and Newton in one sentence, then Ptolemy, Eusebius, Origen and Agricola in the next. Although *A New Theory* utilised a Newtonian notion of gravity, the scientific theories and examples that supported its argument came from chemistry and natural history – not primarily natural philosophy. Focusing on material transformations, effluvial inundations, terrestrial exhalations and magnetic pulses, Wright treats the earth as an organism. Avoiding chronological timescales, he suggests that the earth's life consists of some twelve stages in which it is repeatedly transformed by water and fire, a cosmological periodisation common at the time, echoing the Bible and natural histories like Buffon's *Histoire naturelle* (1749).

Wright was keenly aware of how to market a book. By the time he published An *Original Theory of the Universe*, Newtonian natural philosophy had established itself as a popular literary genre; and this work, with appeals to Georgian tropes of order, mathematical certitude, and a high price tag, was written for an upper-class readership. But *A New Theory* was different. Whereas his earlier publications gave a macroscopic narrative of astronomical order, his later work turns to the relatively microscopic issue of the earth's formation and transformation. Though the other side of the same cosmological coin, it had little relevance for an upmarket audience interested in natural analogues of the social order and which usually knew nothing about the material theories used to explain volcanoes, tides and minerals. To distribute his ideas, Wright, therefore, had to turn to a different medium. Scholars of the time, metropolitan and provincial alike, often wrote up complicated discussions of natural phenomena as manuscript 'books' and 'pamphlets' for circulation amongst friends, colleagues, students and foreign correspondents. Although the circulation routes of such texts in the north of England have yet to be determined, Wright's correspondence lists show that he had assembled an extensive network of former students and intellectual interlocutors – many of whom were women – and it is they who formed the most likely audience for *A New Theory*.

M. D. Eddy

Allan, Bewick and a Dead Giraffe?

38

Thomas Pennant, *History of quadrupeds.* 2nd edition. Vol.1.

London: printed for B. White, 1781.
p.[2], xxiv, 161, [1]. Extra-illustrated copy. 8°. 240 x 200 mm.

Provenance: George Allan's copy, revised and annotated by him with additional plates, including woodcuts by Thomas Bewick.

SC 01643

George Allan of Blackwell Grange, Darlington (1736–1800), is best known as a Durham antiquary. The records that he collected and passed to his friend William Hutchinson underpinned the latter's *History and antiquities of the County Palatine of Durham*, and the two men are fittingly portrayed together in the engraved frontispiece to that work. Allan exemplifies the eighteenth century antiquary, in that his interests were far broader than history, heraldry and archaeology. In 1791 he purchased the natural history museum belonging to Marmaduke Tunstall, of Wycliffe, Co. Durham. Allan had already persuaded his friend Thomas Bewick to spend two months there, producing work that would lead to his *History of British birds.* Allan worked on the organisation and cataloguing of these specimens, which after his death were acquired by the Literary and Philosophical Society of Newcastle and became the foundation of the Hancock Museum.

Allan established a private press, printing editions of his own research work – records of local foundations, historical documents, and more ephemeral pieces. He also did printing for his friends, including several pieces for Thomas Pennant, the writer and naturalist (1726–98), indicating a close link between the owner and the author of this work that is confirmed by their correspondence. Allan recommended Bewick to Pennant, although in the event both men produced their own books on quadrupeds.

Now best known for his correspondence with Gilbert White (whose brother, Benjamin, published this book), Pennant was in the network of writers who were refining the classification of the natural world. Although he corresponded with Linnaeus, Pennant did not concur with him. His preface to *Quadrupeds* shows the then-fluid state of systematics: he discusses and combines the theories of Ray, Klein, Buffon and Linnaeus to produce his own classification schemata.

This volume illustrates the antiquary at work. In his interleaved copy, Allan meticulously added all the changes made in the third edition, plus appropriate illustrations. Bewick sent him proofs from his work, as thirty-six engravings from his *Quadrupeds* have been added to this copy of Pennant. Neither of Pennant's earlier editions included a picture of the giraffe, although Allan added one by Johann Ihle which gives the 'camelopard' a skin covered in small leopard-like spots. Bewick adds more, squarer spots, but Allan commends the engraving (by Peter Mazell) in the 3rd edition for recording the larger, squarer pattern of the markings. The giraffe is one of the very few engravings in Bewick's *Quadrupeds* recorded in three different states, suggesting that it caused him some trouble. It is an uncharacteristically awkward beast, lacking the usual grace of Bewick's creatures; the bends in the neck suggest a dead model.

The University Library owns Allan's personal copies of several of his works, which he printed then corrected and expanded. Extra-illustrated books are vulnerable: the more valuable plates are removed for sale, and the remnants discarded. We have three damaged volumes of Allan's copy of Camden's *Britannia* (originally in twenty-eight volumes, but broken up after 1954) and this single volume from a probable four. The motto Allan prefixed to many of his works seems apt: 'Gather up the fragments that remain' (John 6.12).

Richard Higgins

There is a fine engraving in the 3d Edition, whereby these Animals do not appear to be spotted as usually drawn, but the Skin is marked in Squares as if covered with a Net.

The height of that killed by Mr Patterson was only 15 feet. The head is of an uniform reddish brown: the Neck, back, & sides, outsides of the Shoulders and thighs varied with large tessellated, dull rust colored marks of a square form, with white septaria, or narrow divisions: on the sides the marks are less regular: the belly & legs whitish, faintly spotted: the part of the tail next to the body, is covered with short smooth hairs, & the trunk is very slender: towards the end, the hairs are very long, black and coarse; & forming a great tuft hanging far beyond the tip of the trunk: the hoofs are cloven, and 9 inches broad, and black. This Animal wants the spurious hoofs.

The Female has four teats. Mr Paterson saw Six of these Animals together; possibly they might have been the Male and Female, with their four young.

It is very difficult to distinguish this Animal at a distance, for when standing they look like a decayed tree by reason of their form, so are passed by, & by that deception escape.

39

SELBY'S BEE-EATER

Selby, Prideaux, *Illustrations of British Ornithology; or Figures of British Birds in Their Full Natural Size*, 2 vols. (vol. 1 in 8 parts, vol. 2 in 11 parts).

Edinburgh: 1821–33.

615 x 480 mm.

Provenance: Bamburgh Library

Bamburgh R. 2–3

Selby – whose first name comes from a seventeenth-century ancestor, Rev. Richard Prideaux of Newcastle (whose will is in Durham University Library) – was a landed gentleman of Twizel House, near Alnwick in Northumberland. He was a keen naturalist and sportsman: at the first hint of a rarity he would be off with his gun to collect it before his neighbours heard about it. There was indeed a maxim 'what's hit is history, but what's missed is mystery'; and in the days before binoculars, killing a creature was an essential precondition for describing and illustrating it. It might well then be eaten.

Selby was a good artist, and these were the great days of sumptuous natural histories. He resolved to publish a book so large that the birds would be depicted life-size; and to make this practicable he learned to etch copper plates, and arranged with Lizars in Edinburgh to print them. Making the etchings from his watercolours was a time-consuming process; we learn that it took him the best part of three weeks to do two of them. Sometimes Lizars were left to finish the process, the colouring being done by hand from a plate tinted by Selby as a pattern.

The book came out in parts, as was customary for costly publications. Subscribers would pay for them as they were delivered, so that receipts for part 1 would pay for the printing of part 2, and so on. When sets were complete, the owners would get them bound up.

The birds were dead, either shot by Selby or by someone else who sent him the skin; and he stuffed them, before posing them stiffly on a studio stump or rock. The glint of their glass eyes he showed as a triangle of white, when apparently a spot was customary. The texture of the feathers is beautifully shown. He packed several species of small birds on to one plate; even those with which he must have been very familiar are formally posed and less lifelike than those of Thomas Bewick's contemporary wood-engravings. Yet their sheer size makes the owls and hawks particularly imposing, and sometimes they are pictured with prey. Plate XLI, reproduced here, depicts a rarity in England: the bee-eater, unusually depicted both on a rock and also in flight, where it looks moderately convincing.

In 1826 Selby met John James Audubon in Edinburgh, where he was negotiating with Lizars to engrave and print the plates for his great work on American birds. Selby was struck by Audubon's animated pictures, taking lessons from him and inviting him to stay. His own plates became livelier thenceforward. In 1839, Durham University awarded him an honorary MA.

David Knight

BEE EATERS EUROPEAN. M&F.

Electoral Reform 1831–2

'Report on the State of the Representation 14 January 1831', a manuscript report to Lord Grey by the Reform Committee of Durham, Russell, Graham and Duncannon, with marginal comments by Grey.

[4] leaves. 320 x 205 mm.

Provenance: the Grey Papers (16th to 20th centuries) were deposited by the 5th Earl Grey (1956), with additional deposits by Mary, baroness Howick, and the 2nd Baron Howick (1962–94).

GRE/B46/1/37

The Grey Papers are one of the richest manuscript resources in Durham. They provide an important source for colonial history, through the documents of the first earl's service in the West Indies in the late eighteenth century, the third earl's period as Colonial Secretary from 1846–52, and the fourth earl's service as Governor General of Canada from 1904–11, as well as through the papers of Evelyn Baring, first Earl of Cromer, and Evelyn Baring, first Baron Howick of Glendale. The first earl was a significant player in the defence of England against Napoleon; his command of the Southern District yields material for the military historian, as well as documents about safeguarding the country against the Nore mutineers in 1797. More military material is found in the papers of his grandson: Henry, the third earl, was Secretary at War from 1830–34. The second earl's lifelong interest in foreign affairs provides another major resource, amplified by the papers of Viscount Ponsonby. Maria, wife of the third earl, kept an extensive diary, and her correspondence with other 'political wives' is complemented by letters from her sister, and also by the letters of Lady Palmer, comtesse de Franqueville. There is also valuable material for the economic historian in the form of the estate papers from Grey family property in Northumberland.

Yet however valuable the other papers, emphasis is rightly given to the second Earl Grey's role in the passing of the 'great' Reform Act of 1832. By the time he succeeded to the earldom in 1807, Charles Grey was already an established politician. Entering Parliament in 1786, he was an early 'Friend of the People,' and maintained his Foxite stance through the tribulations of the French Revolution. He joined the government initially as First Lord of the Admiralty (1806), and subsequently (1806–7) Foreign Secretary, but his ministerial career came to an abrupt halt with the resumption of war. By the end of hostilities Grey was the acknowledged, if at times reluctant, leader of the Whigs; but in 1820, during the years of Tory domination, he came to the conclusion that he would not see Parliamentary Reform in his lifetime. The dramatic change in the political climate that thrust him into the Premiership in 1830 at the age of sixty-six thus produced the triumphant climax to a frustrating political career. A committee consisting of Lords Duncannon and Durham, Lord John Russell and Sir James Graham reported to Cabinet in February 1831 on a plan of reform, though Grey's own conservative approach to the question is apparent, for example, in his annotation of the Committee's proposal to adopt the ballot as part of the scheme (illustrated on the plate): 'My opinion is against this'. A two-year struggle to secure the bill ensued, and though some radicals remained disappointed, Grey was probably correct when he wrote to the north-eastern reformer J. R. Fenwick in November 1831 that his plan of reform 'far exceeded the expectation of the most eager Reformer'. Post-Reform quarrels within the Government (well documented in the collection) led to Grey's disillusionment; and his resignation in 1834 ushered in a bitter old age – dismissing, for example, Lord John Russell (who, with Lord Althorp had steered the Reform Bill through the Commons) as 'a little animal, engrossed by inordinate ambition, of the most narrow and selfish kind'.

Alan Heesom

37/4

R. 9. S 19.
R. 12. S 245 & 381.
My opinion is against this
G.

The Enforcement of Residence
× The Registration of Votes
— The Adoption of Ballot
The encrease of the Numbers of Polling Booths. R. 12. R. 16.
The shortening the duration of the Poll R. 12 –
And the taking the Poll (in Counties) in Hundreds or Divisions.

We finally propose that the duration of Parliament should be limited to Five Years.

We have embodied these arrangements, and other measures of detail connected with them, in Three Bills, The Heads of which we annex to this Report.

Durham
James R. G. Graham
John Russell
Duncannon –

THE UNDERGRADUATE.

A STUDY FOR A SKETCH.

THE UNDERGRADUATE

41

'The Undergraduate. A Study for a Sketch'.

Watercolour with pen and ink by 'Cuthbert Bede' (Edward Bradley); *c.* 1849.
Portfolio containing 65 sketches. This picture: 211 x 192 mm.

Purchased by the library at Hodgsons no. 6 sale, March 1957, lot 250/2.

Add. MS 732/60

Edward Bradley (1827–89), from Kidderminster, was a Durham graduate who left University College in 1849 with a L.Th., having received his B.A. the previous year. He was ordained in 1850, thereafter holding a series of livings in the Midlands. However, whilst at Durham, he had already demonstrated his talents as a novelist and illustrator, adopting the locally-inspired pen-name Cuthbert Bede in 1846 for some verse contributions to *Bentley's Miscellany*. He also produced an undergraduate comic strip *Ye Freshmonne*, set in Durham. An Oxford setting was more marketable though, so the strip appeared in the *Illustrated London News* from the end of 1851 as 'The Adventures of Mr Verdant Green, An Oxford Freshman'. The strip developed into an illustrated and highly successful shilling railway novel of the same title in 1853. With two sequels, 'The Further Adventures of Mr. Verdant Green, an Oxford Undergraduate' (1854) and 'Mr. Verdant Green, Married and Done For' (1857), Bradley's, or rather Cuthbert Bede's, fame was assured. Subsequent works did not have the same lasting impact as the depiction, character and adventures of the comical Verdant Green.

Bradley's papers were dispersed after his death. As a result of subsequent attempts to garner his surviving works in Durham, the University Library has the largest such collection in the UK, and further drawings, watercolours and images are in Durham Castle. From a portfolio of sketches in the library's Additional Manuscripts comes this watercolour of an undergraduate. Not itself published, it bears comparison to Etching '17' of a similar scene in Bradley's first independent publication, *College Life* (1849–50), a series of etchings of life at Oxford, and occasionally Durham. The genre of the comfortably recumbent undergraduate, legs crossed, enjoying his smoke, appears also in the Verdant Green novels. The location here is not recognisably either Oxford or Durham. However the message is clear: this is a sporting man. The academic gown and mortar board are discarded on one side, a torn copy of Euclid lies on the floor on the other. Books are in the bookcase, almost out of the picture; the table is adorned rather with a beer tankard, a bottle of Bass, a decanter and a copy of *Bell's Life* (the sporting paper). On the wall a 'Hunting Fixtures' notice intrudes between the Thirty-Nine Articles and 'Kings Israel Judah'. Also on the wall are guns, rapiers, boxing gloves, an antlered head and a picture of a plump lady. A small dog adoringly admires its master. The overall style of the work, and of the furniture in particular, suggests that the watercolour may have been done during Bradley's time at Durham. No matter how accurately the image portrays contemporary undergraduates at Durham and Oxford, and despite its limited technical accomplishment, Bradley's caricature provides a vital, irreverent insight into the university's early years.

M. M. N. Stansfield

Kilvert's Diary

42

Francis Kilvert, manuscript notebook entitled by the author, 'Journal. No. 4. 1870. From July 19th. to August 6th. Cornwall'.

180 p. 177 x 110 mm.

Provenance: presented to William Plomer by Mrs Essex Hope (née Smith), Kilvert's niece, on 16 September 1958.

Plomer MS 454

The journal kept by the Victorian curate Francis Kilvert (1840–79) is one of the most admired and best-loved of all English diaries. It first became known in 1938–41 when William Plomer, then a reader for Capes, caused a literary sensation by publishing three volumes of extracts from the manuscripts. The Diary's history is extraordinary. It filled twenty-eight to thirty notebooks at the time of Kilvert's death, five weeks after his marriage. His widow Elizabeth removed, for personal reasons, all the notebooks covering two lengthy periods; and either she or later family owners carried out numerous more minor acts of censorship, excising passages and pages. The twenty-two remaining notebooks eventually passed to Kilvert's niece, Mrs Essex Hope. Plomer's edited selection printed in all about one-third of the surviving Diary. Its success was so great that there were widespread calls for a complete edition; but at some date before 1955 Mrs Essex Hope apparently destroyed all the original notebooks except three. These three she gave away, one of them to William Plomer. They are consecutive, and date from 1870, the first year of the Diary; two are now in the National Library of Wales, while Plomer's notebook was bequeathed to Durham University Library along with his other literary papers.

The Durham notebook is a deliberately self-contained account of an eventful three-week holiday that Kilvert spent in Cornwall from 19 July to 6 August 1870, staying with his close friends William and Emma Hockin. Kilvert's account of Cornwall is unforgettable and highly individual, as he and his hosts accomplish astonishing feats of energetic tourism. Everything he writes is marked with his own delightful personality, with his irrepressible humour, his infatuations, enthusiasms and prejudices, his alert observation, close engagement with the humblest people he meets, and his art of capturing precisely those unexpected details that bring a personality alive and transform an otherwise familiar scene. The Plomer notebook, uniquely, has escaped all destructive censorship, and contains some of the most unexpected and explicit moments of self-revelation to have survived. There is clear evidence of Kilvert's growing infatuation with the beautiful, charming and lively Emma Hockin – no surprise, for he was always helplessly susceptible to pretty young women. But it is a surprise when on Sunday 24 July, the quietest day of the entire holiday, as Kilvert and the Hockins talk over coffee in the summerhouse before Evensong, the diarist suddenly adds: '"Aside the devil turned &c. &c." – Ah, how intelligible' (see illustration). The reference is to *Paradise Lost*, IV, 502–11, as Satan gazes in furious jealousy at the physical happiness of Adam and Eve, and is consumed with frustrated lust and unfulfilled desire. This brief personal note is immediately followed by a comic picture of the local clergyman; but it perhaps gives a hint as to what some of the lost parts of the Diary might have contained. Plomer omitted the whole day's entry from his edition, along with two-thirds of the rest of this notebook.

Richard Maber

Sunday. 24. July. We went to Church twice morning & evening at 11 & 6.30. The way to Church is very pleasant – up the Shrubbery through the flower garden & by a greenhouse. into outer kitchen garden. then across the top lane by a private walk through private door into the Church yard. The Church has a fine old grey tower with pinnacles. & a noble high flight of many broad granite steps leads up to the Church yard gate. The Chancel is restored – the nave is still churchwarden's Gothic. There is a very nice pretty pulpit hanging which Mrs. H. made & gave. Very few people in Church. The heat excessive. The clergyman Mr. Hawkins read some part of the service very fast – much too fast – especially the Litany. but preached a good sermon.

The privacy. quietness & deep peacefulness of this place is very delightful particularly on Sundays.

In the afternoon we had coffee out in the summer house & sat there talking till the heat of the day had abated. "Beside the devil turned as a —" Ah how intelligible.

In the evening we went to Church again at 6.30. As we left Church the clergyman rushed out after us in his cassock. Mrs. H & I had gone on before. but he buttonholed H. & proposed calling on me tomorrow. To my great relief H. rather discouraged his intentions than otherwise. by saying that he would not find us at home as we should be touring about all the way.

slurring in English of unaccented syllables; which is a beauty of the language, so that ~~and~~ only misguided people say Dev-*il*, six-*pence* distinctly; still even this is not essential. The accented syllable then is the one of which the ~~nature~~ is ~~well brought out~~, whatever may become of the others. When the others are as well brought ~~out~~ then, but this is seldom, happens that which you so acutely point out, that the mind, as ~~in~~ it does to the tick tock of a clock, supplies ~~a~~ for a ~~certain spell~~ while that difference which has ceased to be marked ~~really~~ outwardly. And this is clearly seen in singing ~~music~~; for, however smoothly and equally the notes are sung, if the accent of the syllable does not fall on the accent, primary or secondary, of the bar — though in fact neither the note nor the syllable sung to it were ~~be~~ any louder than the rest — the effect is intolerable; if for instance instead of

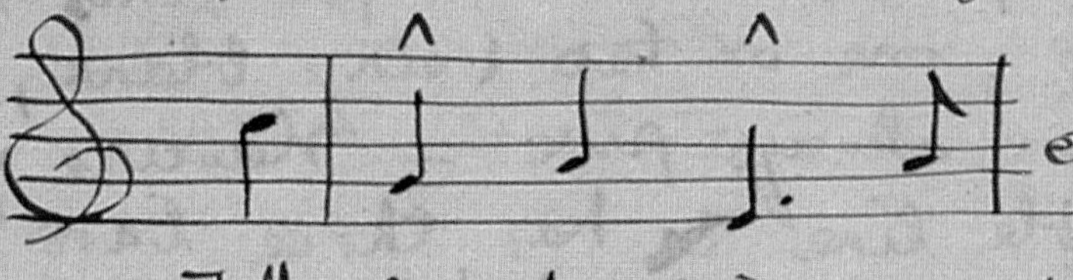

we made it

I put aside of course ~~reverse~~ syncopations and other calculated effects, as in all art.

It only remains to say that the stress, the *ictus*, of our verse is founded on and in the beginning the very same as the stress which is our accent. In fact in smooth and simple and especially in strongly marked lyrics

Gerard Manley Hopkins

43

Gerard Manley Hopkins, letters to Coventry Patmore.

22 letters; 1883–8.

Provenance: collection of Claude Colleer Abbott (d. 1971); given to the library by his literary executors.

Abbott MSS 181–202

Gerard Manley Hopkins (1844–89) was not only one of the great poets of the nineteenth century, but a most remarkable letter writer. His letters contain the observations of an acute and sensitive critical mind, and are probably (after those of Keats) the most valuable commentary on poets and poetic theory of that era. Some of the most interesting are those to the poet Coventry Patmore (1823–96) who, like Hopkins, was a convert to Roman Catholicism.

Twenty-two letters of Hopkins to Patmore are contained in the Abbott Collection. Claude Colleer Abbott (1889–1971), professor of English at the University, 1932–54, and the editor of Hopkins's letters, published those in this collection in his *Further Letters of Gerard Manley Hopkins including his Correspondence with Coventry Patmore* (1938); his edition has stood the test of time remarkably well. Abbott does not say how the letters came into his possession.

Hopkins met Patmore in 1883 whilst teaching at Stonyhurst when the latter visited the College in July for Speech Day. The correspondence was quickly begun, and proceeded with astonishing energy and intensity, especially on Hopkins's part. Hopkins was anxious to draw Patmore's attention to the work of his friends, Robert Bridges and Richard Watson Dixon (Bridges had recently published *Prometheus the Firegiver* and Dixon *Mano: a Poetical History*); Patmore was keen to show Hopkins his poetry. On 14 September Hopkins acknowledged receipt of four volumes of *Poems* (1879), following this up on 23 September with detailed criticisms of Patmore's most important poem, 'The Angel in the House'. These are numbered from 1 to 32, and over them Patmore has written in pencil, either crossing them out or writing 'Done' when he agreed with what Hopkins had written. Hopkins wrote with more criticisms on 24 September, and again in October and November, often in great detail and with obvious engagement and enthusiasm.

Hopkins's freedom in this correspondence is rare for him. The reason was probably that he was thrilled to find another Roman Catholic poet with whom he could share his views on poetry. Patmore had theories on prosody: his *Amelia, Tamerton Church Tower &c* (1878) contained a preface on English metre. Hopkins found fault with the poems, sometimes expressing himself strongly, but Patmore responded graciously: 'Your careful and subtle fault-finding is the greatest praise my poetry has ever received.'

The originals are in Hopkins's characteristic hand – upright, some italic influence, and Greek deltas. An expert in hand-writing would probably observe the same combination of idiosyncrasy and awkward beauty that is found in his poetry; to come face to face with them is to feel wonderfully close to one of the most original poetic minds of the nineteenth century.

J. R. Watson

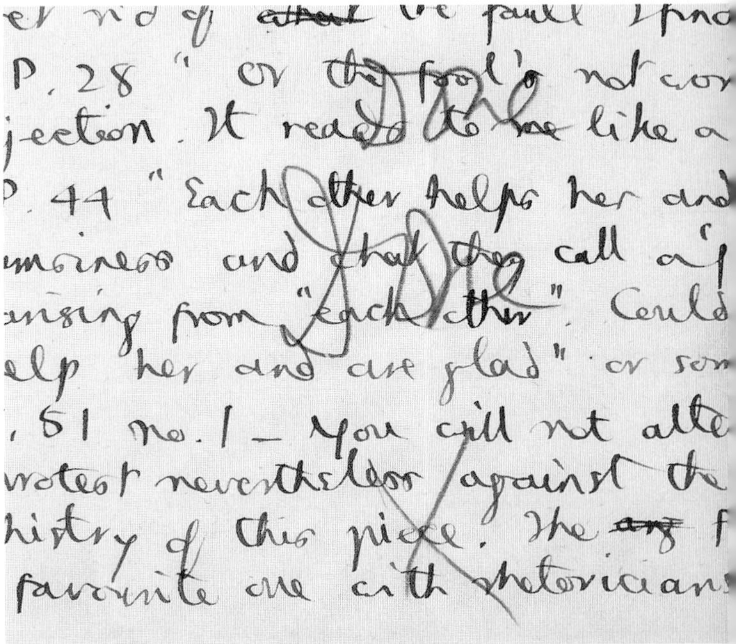
P. 28 " or the fool's not con-
jection. It reads to me like a
P. 44 " Each other helps her and
and that they call a
from "each other". Could
her and are glad" · or som
no. 1 – You will not alte
protest nevertheless against the
history of this piece. The
favourite one with rhetoricians

A Khartoum Currency

44

Banknote issued by General Gordon during the siege of Khartoum, 1884–5.

62 x 107 mm

Provenance: M. W. Parr

SAD 11/9/4

Durham's Sudan Archive was founded in 1957, the year after Sudanese independence, and has become one of the world's most important repositories for material on the country. It includes the papers of over 300 colonial administrators, missionaries, soldiers, and others. Although its focus is the period between 1898 and 1955, the archive also holds material relating to the British military campaigns of the 1880s and 90s, to post-independence Sudan, as well as to other countries in Africa and the Middle East.

For those brought up around 1900, Charles George Gordon was a quintessential imperial hero. He was 'Gordon Pasha', 'Chinese Gordon', 'Gordon of Khartoum', whose exploits were moulded into a one-dimensional tale of valour and patriotism that would shape the outlook of boys long before he was immortalised by Charlton Heston in *Khartoum* (1966). Opprobrium was heaped upon Bloomsbury biographer Lytton Strachey when, in his *Eminent Victorians* (1918), he deemed Gordon a 'contradictious person—even a little off his head, perhaps, though a hero'.

Appointed by Gladstone to help evacuate Egyptian garrisons from the Sudan in the face of the jihad of the Islamic leader Muhammad Ahmad (better known as the Mahdi), Gordon instead reached Khartoum in February 1884 and attempted to win back areas from the Mahdists. However his proposal for more British troops to be sent to the Sudan was rejected by London, and a siege began. The telegraph line to Egypt was cut on 12 March and, once the Mahdi himself had arrived, establishing headquarters near to the city, the situation became more grave. Gordon's coffers began to empty quickly, as he was forced to pay and provision his army, and to feed the civilian population of the city. So, taking matters into his own hands, from April 1884 onwards he issued a series of banknotes that could, he promised, be redeemed six months hence in Cairo – the pledge inscribed in Arabic across the centre of the note. Gordon personally signed some 50,000 of the 91,000 or so notes, which were issued in varying denominations of both piastres and pounds. Such a course of action is not unparalleled: the Prussians had issued notes when Kolberg had been besieged during the Napoleonic Wars in 1807, as did Baden Powell when the Boers surrounded Mafikeng (Mafeking) during the Second Boer War.

The currency smoothed the functioning of Khartoum society as far as was possible in such circumstances because, despite his efforts, Gordon knew that there was no way out unless a relief force be sent. Gladstone, who remained intent on evacuating the Sudan, initially rejected calls from Queen Victoria and the British press for such an expedition. The Prime Minister eventually relented, only for Wolseley's relief expedition to arrive two days too late. The Mahdists had captured Khartoum in the early hours of 26 January 1885, killing Gordon and his weakened troops along with other inhabitants. This ushered in thirteen years during which the country was an Islamic state – until Lord Kitchener and General Wingate's military campaigns led to the establishment of the Anglo-Egyptian Sudan in 1899.

Christopher Prior

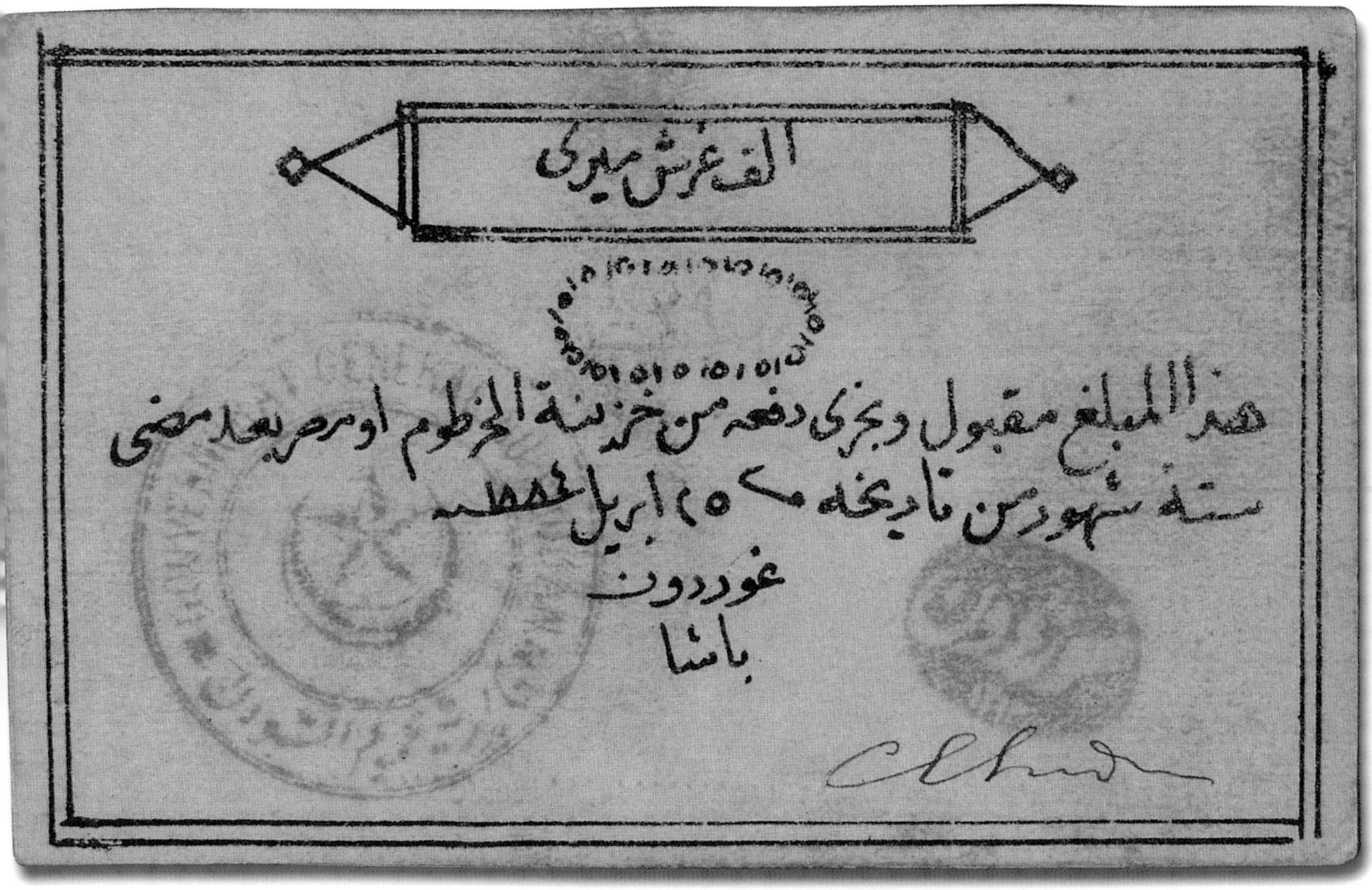
الف غرش ميرى
هذا المبلغ مقبول ويجرى دفعه من خزينة الخرطوم او مصر بعد مضى
ستة شهور من تاريخه ٢٥ ابريل ١٨٨٤
غوردون
باشا

45

BAIRSTOW'S *WATERS OF BABYLON*

Edward Cuthbert Bairstow (1874–1946), *By the waters of Babylon (Psalm 137), set to music for tenor solo, chorus and orchestra. Autograph signed and dated 'Ed. C. Bairstow/28.viii.1900'. Orchestration*: 2 Fl; 2 Ob; 2 Cl in B flat; 2 Bn; 2 Hn in G; 2Hn in D; 2Tr in E flat; 2 Ten Tromb; Bass Tromb; Timp; Str.

78 p. 24-stave manuscript. 274 x 375 mm

Exercise submitted for the degree of Mus.D. at Durham University.

UMU 144

Initially, music degrees at Durham University were purely honorary and were mainly reserved for prominent composers of church music such as Sir Frederick Ouseley (Mus.D. 1856), professor of Music at Oxford; John Bacchus Dykes (Mus.D. 1862), one time precentor of Durham Cathedral (1849–62) and vicar of St Oswald's; and John Stainer (D.Mus. 1885), organist of St Paul's Cathedral – though Sir George Grove, soon to be famous for his musical dictionary, received a DCL (1875).

In 1890 the University began written examinations in the wake of their introduction at London (1879); other institutions such as Edinburgh, Manchester and Birmingham were soon to follow Durham's example. Philip Armes, organist of Durham Cathedral, was appointed 'resident examiner' and first Professor of Music (1897) and it was he, with the assistance of Sir John Stainer, who formulated the content of the degrees of Mus.B. and Mus.D.

For the Mus.B. it was necessary to pass two examinations (which consisted of questions in harmony and counterpoint, form, the history of music and the study of prescribed scores); the candidate was also required to submit a choral composition that showed proficiency in choral techniques (including a five-part fugue), a solo aria and accompaniment for string orchestra. These technical strictures can be observed in Edward Bairstow's Mus.B. exercise *O how amiable*, a setting of Psalm 84 examined by Armes, Stainer and George Garrett (organist of St John's College, Cambridge) and part of his successful supplication in 1894. The Mus.D. required written examinations in eight-part harmony and counterpoint, fugue, canon and imitation, instrumentation, form, history of music, acoustics and a 'knowledge of the standard classical works', along with an exercise for eight-part chorus, soli and orchestra, including a full orchestral overture. This is exemplified in Bairstow's Mus.D. exercise, *By the waters of Babylon (Psalm 137)*, submitted in 1900, in the substantial overture and opening eight-part chorus 'By the waters of Babylon' (the transition between these two movements is illustrated), the tenor aria, 'If I forget thee, O Jerusalem' and the grand finale, 'Remember the children of Edom', subtitled 'Introduction, Fugue, and Choral Recitative'. The degree was examined by Armes, George J. Bennett (organist of Lincoln Cathedral) and Sir J. Frederick Bridge (organist of Westminster Abbey and Gresham Professor of Music).

Durham's collection of degree exercises is extensive, and among its successful supplicants were Walter Carroll (Mus.B. 1891), Walter Alcock (Mus.B. 1896; Mus.D. 1905), John Ireland (Mus.B. 1908) – with an attractive setting of words selected from Psalm 42 – and Malcolm Sargent. Sargent successfully supplicated for his Mus.B. in 1914 at the age of nineteen, with his cantata *The Cloud*, a setting of Shelley's poem of that name. In 1919, after brief service in the army, Sargent supplicated for the Mus.D. with another setting of Shelley's words, this time the well-known *Ode to a Skylark*. He is reputed to be the youngest successful candidate for this degree in the country.

After appointments at Wigan and Leeds parish churches, Edward Bairstow took up his last organist post – at York Minster in 1913. While he was there, he succeeded Joseph Bridge as professor of music at Durham (1929), a position he held until his death in May 1946. Thereafter, with the institution of the new B.A. degree, residence for the Professor of Music became mandatory.

Jeremy Dibble

27.
No II. Chorus. "By the waters of Babylon.
Flauti
Oboi
Clarinetti
Tymp
Violin 1
Violin 2
Viola
Adagio
Chorus
And wept. When we re-
By the wa-ters of Babylon we sat down
When we re-mem-ber'd
Celli
C. Bassi

46

Ali Dinar, last Sultan of Darfur

Sword of Ali Dinar, last Sultan of Darfur. Gold hilt with multi-coloured tassle and carved metal blade, the blade probably of Sollingen manufacture, the hilt probably of local Darfur manufacture. The blade is decorated with various inscriptions and magical formulae, one of which includes the Sultan's name and the date 1321 [1903/04]. The Sultan's name is repeated on the hilt with the date 1331 [1913].

Provenance: J.A. Gillan, who as Assistant Political and Intelligence Officer, Darfur Expeditionary Force, was present at the Sultan's death.

SAD G//S 628/1

Coins of Sultan Ali Dinar of Darfur, produced from Darfur iron, various dates, 1899–1916.

Provenance: H. A. MacMichael, Political Officer, Darfur Expeditionary Force, 1916.

SAD G//S 5/1

When, half a century ago, Richard Hill began to solicit material for the Sudan Archive, that most diplomatic of historians received with equanimity not only documents and photographs but also an array of odds and ends accumulated by former officials of the Sudan Government and others. These ranged from museum pieces to souvenirs and mementos whose value was apparent only to their consigners. Hill would not risk losing a trove of Arabic manuscripts by rejecting a petrified ostrich egg.

Some of the most interesting and varied materials in the Archive relate to the life and times of Ali Dinar Zakariyya Muhammad al-Fadl (*c.* 1865–1916), the last sultan of Darfur. The Fur state, with its capital at El Fasher, had dominated the western marches of the Sudan for over two centuries when it was conquered in 1874 by al-Zubayr Pasha Rahma Mansur, the Ja'ali Arab trader who had already carved out a commercial empire in the southern Sudan. Ensuing Egyptian rule was brief and chaotic, and Darfur fell easily to the Mahdi in the early 1880s. Following the Anglo-Egyptian extinction of the Mahdist State in 1898, Ali Dinar re-established autonomy in Darfur and managed to hold out against the encroaching French and British empires until the First World War. Darfur's subsequent experience of colonial rule was thus one of the briefest in Africa, and the current (2007) crisis there illustrates – among other things – both the continuity and the change since the days of Ali Dinar.

Museum pieces, such as those illustrated here, hint at the nature and extent of the Fur sultanate during its final phase. Heir to a multi-ethnic empire built on long-distance trade, Ali Dinar and his chiefs enjoyed a ramshackle panoply of varied provenance, including local manufacture. A number of imported swords survived as trophies. The sultan's coinage, as both attribute of sovereignty and supplement to imported coins and local media of exchange, is of similar historical interest.

Martin Daly

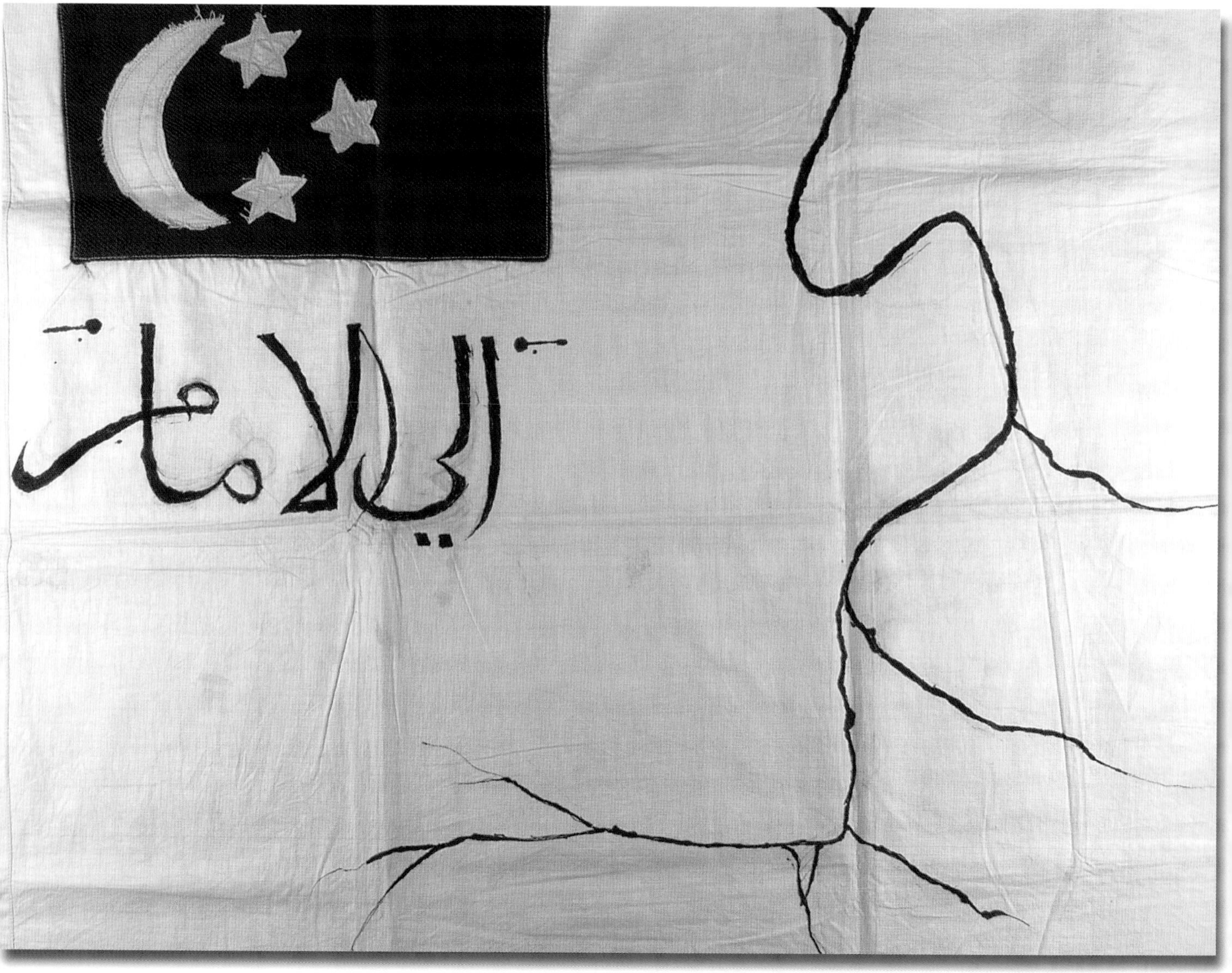
الى الامام

The Early Days of Sudanese Nationalism

47

Photograph of leaders of the White Flag League posing in front of their banner. Taken in Khartoum, Sudan, 1924.

84 x 114 mm.

Provenance: Judge R. Wedd.

SAD 474/10/1

Flag of the White Flag League, seized in the first Khartoum demonstrations, 23 June 1924.

Provenance: Judge R. Wedd.

SAD 475/3

During and immediately after the First World War, parts of Egypt were awash with nationalist protest. The Wafd, led by Saad Zaghlul, demanded national self-determination for the country which had been occupied by the British since 1882 and then held as a protectorate from 1914. In 1922, the British finally issued a declaration of Egypt's independence. This independence, however, was qualified by the reservation of four issues for future settlement – one of which was the status of the Sudan.

Heavily influenced by events in Egypt, the White Flag League was established in 1924. The League was led by 'Ali 'Abd al-Latif (pictured, second from right). He was joined by (from left to right in the photograph, excepting al-Latif): 'Ubaid al-Hajj al-Amin, Salih 'Abd al-Qadir and Hasan Sharif. The aim of the League was to effect the 'Unity of the Nile Valley'. The flag (actually a pillow case) shows the course of the Nile as a means of symbolizing such unity. The political ramifications were never fully elaborated, but the aim appears to have been for the Sudan to place itself under the guidance of Egypt's nationalist politicians and her monarch, King Fu'ad, as a means of strengthening the move towards independence, the alliance between the two countries being an expedient to undercut the 'Sudan for the Sudanese' programme as espoused by more moderate nationalists such as 'Sayyid 'Abd al-Rahman al-Mahdi, the son of the Mahdi.

al-Latif was scorned by the British as an educated African who had lost touch with his 'tribal' roots and, though the influence of the League was limited, the British were caught by surprise when it instigated anti-imperial demonstrations during the spring and summer of 1924. al-Latif was arrested in July; then in August, the Egyptian Army Railway Battalion in Atbara rose in a revolt which was put down by British force. Matters came to a head in November 1924 when Sir Lee Stack, the Governor-General of the Sudan and the Sirdar of the Egyptian Army, was assassinated in Cairo. This gave the British the necessary excuse to order all Egyptian troops to leave the Sudan. On 27 November, members of the Eleventh Sudanese Battalion, showing solidarity with the Egyptians, ignored British demands to lay down arms – leading to a gun battle on the streets of Khartoum. The revolt was crushed, the Egyptians were shipped out, and al-Latif was consigned to a psychiatric hospital (effectively imprisoned) in Cairo where he eventually died in 1948. The British felt that the situation was relatively stable – but this was not to last.

Christopher Prior

The *English Hymnal* annotated by its Editor

48

The English Hymnal.

Oxford: University Press. London: Henry Frowde, Amen Corner [1906].

628 p. 141 x 97 mm.

Provenance: Percy Dearmer's proof copy; given by Mrs G. Warr.

Pratt Green X 783.9 F0 ENG

The *English Hymnal*, published in 1906, was probably the single most influential hymn-book of the twentieth century. It was edited by a committee led by Percy Dearmer (1867–1936), then vicar of St Mary the Virgin, Primrose Hill, London, who made the inspired choice of the young Ralph Vaughan Williams (1872–1958) as music editor. Dearmer himself, who also compiled *Songs of Praise*, was undoubtedly the most important hymn-book editor of the century.

The library's hymnology collection, generously endowed by the Pratt Green Trust using royalties from the Methodist hymn-writer Fred Pratt Green (1903–2000), contains an undated copy of the words-only edition of EH, marked on the title page 'Confidential. Proof copy. Sheets not yet finally corrected'. Inside the front cover is a list (dated 1924) of other hymn-books in which the hymns had appeared. After the first list, various coloured inks were used in an additional list, which is itself supplemented by three entries in red, ending 'In New Book (Songs of Praise)'.

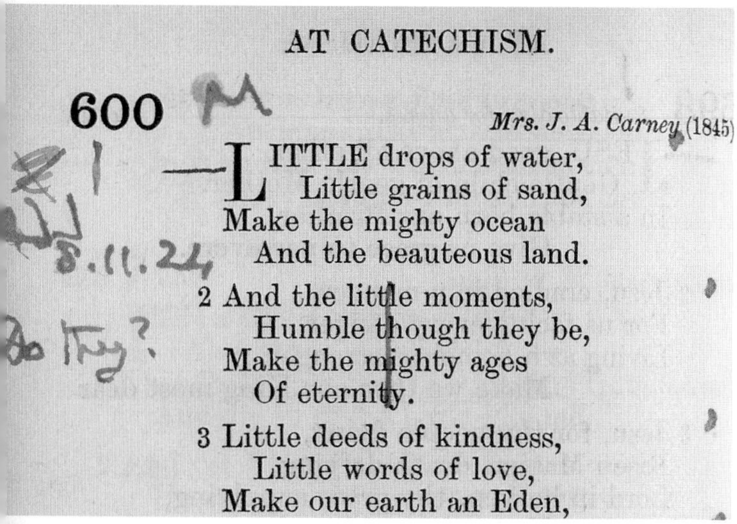
AT CATECHISM.

600 *Mrs. J. A. Carney* (1845)

LITTLE drops of water,
Little grains of sand,
Make the mighty ocean
And the beauteous land.

2 And the little moments,
Humble though they be,
Make the mighty ages
Of eternity.

3 Little deeds of kindness,
Little words of love,
Make our earth an Eden,

The book is Percy Dearmer's working copy for a possible revision of *EH*, probably dating from 1925 (the year of *Songs of Praise*) or shortly thereafter. It is a record of which hymns had been successful, judged by the use made of them in other books between 1906 and 1924, together with further suggestions for amendment. In the event, this work was unused because the committee of the revised *EH* of 1933 took the decision not to alter the texts of the 1906 book. Nevertheless, the copy is a valuable record of Dearmer's thinking, and also of the character of the original *EH*: thus the Office Hymns 'from the Epiphany till Lent', numbered 56–69, were (with one exception) found in no other books. Similarly, the hymns on martyrs, confessors, 'for a virgin', and 'for a matron', numbered 180–93, appear in no other books, and many of the hymns for saints, from 213–37, are rarely found elsewhere.

Sometimes Dearmer scored through verses. He was notably harsh on the hymns of F. W. Faber, marking 'alter' against the first verse of no 161, which ends 'Have mercy on us, worms of earth,/ Most holy Trinity' (Dearmer's aversion to 'worms' is cheerfully chronicled in *Songs of Praise Discussed*, 1933). Occasionally he wrote 'No' against a hymn, or crossed it out entirely. One was Cowper's 'Hark my soul! It is the Lord', probably because it was thought too intimate for congregational use; another was Albert Midlane's 'There's a friend for little children'.

Once he allowed himself a comment. Verse 2 of Mrs Carney's 'Little drops of water' is: 'And the little moments, / Humble though they be, / Make the mighty ages / Of eternity' – on which he commented: 'Do they?'

His conclusions are found in the recto of the final page: 'Write to papers, asking opinions, saying we propose to omit from among: General (those unmarked here) / All Mission (Except those marked) / Among Catechism those not marked'.

The book is a unique copy which gives a valuable insight into the mind of a great hymnologist.

J. R. Watson

THE

ENGLISH HYMNAL

Confidential.
Proof copy.
Sheets not yet
finally corrected

OXFORD
PRINTED AT THE UNIVERSITY PRESS
LONDON: HENRY FROWDE
AMEN CORNER

W. H. Auden's *Poems* Presented to his Fiancée

49

W. H. Auden, *Poems*.

[Hampstead/Oxford]: S.H.S., 1928.

[6], 3–37 p. 125 x 95 mm.

Provenance: author's presentation copy to Sheilah M. Richardson (dated 26.2.29), who gave it, plus two photographs of Auden, to Miss H. M. Trudgian in 1947, by whom given to the Library in 1951.

SB 2052

W. H. Auden's *Poems* is one of the rarest, as well as one of the smallest, collections of modern poetry. The book was published in striking dark orange covers during the summer vacation of 1928, when Auden and his fellow-poet Stephen Spender were students at Oxford. Spender later recalled how he offered to print his friend's poems on a small hand-printing set, but the machinery (and his patience) broke down and the work was eventually completed by the Holywell Press in Oxford. The inking is uneven and the page numbers are sometimes poorly set, but the quality of the printing improves from page 23 onwards.

In his autobiography, *World Within World* (1951), Spender claims that only thirty copies were published, and it would appear that fewer than twenty of these have survived. B. C. Bloomfield lists fifteen copies in his Auden bibliography (1973), including copies owned by Christopher Isherwood and Cyril Connolly; a further copy, owned by the novelist Edward Upward, is now in the possession of the British Library. The Durham copy was presented by Auden to Sheilah Richardson, a nurse to whom he was briefly engaged in 1928–29. Shortly after the publication of the book, Auden spent a year in Berlin that would prove decisive in his maturing as a writer, but the 1928 poems establish many of his familiar stylistic traits and thematic motifs.

There are twenty poems in the book, although the first is a sequence of eight short lyric pieces. The poems are often cryptic, precocious and introspective, but they are also distinctively 'Audenesque' in their challenging, allusive style and in their exploration of remote and isolated landscapes. From the beginning, Auden is drawn to abandoned places of work that have a special picturesque charm: 'Sheds crumbling stone by stone, / The awkward waterwheel / Of a deserted mine'. Poem VI, later titled 'The Watershed', lingers over the 'dismantled washing-floors' and 'Snatches of tramline' that recall the lead-mining industry in the North Pennines, close to Auden's cherished Alston Moor. Poem XV, later 'The Secret Agent', is alive with political and sexual intrigue, and it also shows Auden experimenting with the sonnet (a favourite form in later years). Several poems were revised and adopted as part of a longer work, 'Paid on Both Sides: A Charade', published by T. S. Eliot in *The Criterion* in January 1930. The modifications that Auden made to his 1928 poems offer valuable insights into his methods of composition and revision. The dawn landscapes and guarded frontiers of the early writings might seem to evoke an uncertain and insecure creativity, but they also convey the impression of a prodigiously gifted poet on the verge of a new decade and a new literary movement. The imaginative reach and virtuosity of these early Auden poems is evidence enough to justify Spender's famous remark that 'The 1930s began in 1928'.

Stephen Regan

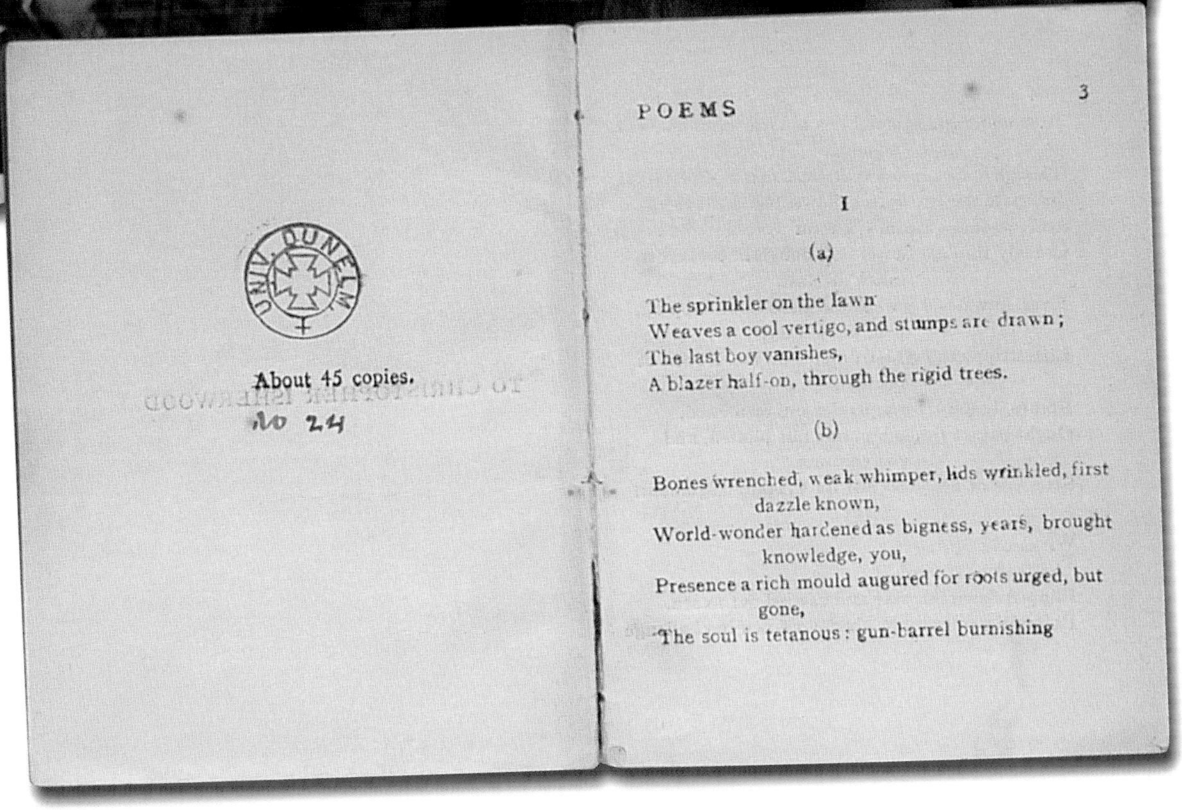

About 45 copies.

no 24

I

(a)

The sprinkler on the lawn
Weaves a cool vertigo, and stumps are drawn;
The last boy vanishes,
A blazer half-on, through the rigid trees.

(b)

Bones wrenched, weak whimper, lids wrinkled, first
dazzle known,
World-wonder hardened as bigness, years, brought
knowledge, you,
Presence a rich mould augured for roots urged, but
gone,
The soul is tetanous: gun-barrel burnishing

DINKA MOTHER AND CHILD AT SHAMBE

50

Sudan photographic collection.

Item date: *c.* 1940. 380 x 270 mm.

Provenance: Dr J. F. E. Bloss.

SAD 705/6/7

Few collections within the University Library's Sudan Archive better exemplify the varied interests and abilities of British officials in the Sudan than the photographs of Dr J.F.E. Bloss (d. 1982). While the Political Service (the famous administrative elite of the Sudan civil service) dominated contemporary popular perceptions of the Anglo-Egyptian Condominium, it was the technical personnel who built from scratch the foundations of modern social services in the Sudan – as elsewhere in the Empire. The Medical Service (and allied departments, including Midwifery and Nursing, and the Wellcome and Stack laboratories) achieved particular success: the daunting challenges of the Sudan's heterogeneous population, a catalogue of endemic and epidemic diseases, the special problems of internal migration and the trans-Sudan pilgrimage routes to Mecca, along with chronic under-funding, were met with perseverance, great organizational skill, and impressive innovation.

While Dr Bloss played his appointed role in these developments – a career well-documented in his papers, published reports and articles, unpublished memoirs, and in the accounts of others, all kept in the Durham Archive – it is his achievement in photography that is celebrated today (and is likely to be of increasing importance in the future). The Bloss collection of about 1,800 photographs is a relatively small portion of the Archive's total holding of more than 40,000 images; moreover, the thousands of photographs dating from the 1880s and possibly earlier are a treasure trove that sometimes provides the only 'accounts' we have of certain important events, the only impressions of historical personages, and the best record of long-term environmental and cultural change. The Bloss Collection, however, is important both for its historical value and its artistic merit. The photograph reproduced here, of a Dinka mother and child taken at Shambe in the 1940s, is but one example. Like an Old Master painting, not only is it visually stunning, it is also a record of a lost society, one that has since been mutilated. Other Bloss photographs similarly record features of local culture as diverse as personal adornment and hunting techniques, along with environmental conditions over a wide range of the Sudan's varied landscape. Since the 1950s the Southern Sudan has experienced constant unrest and long periods of open warfare: millions were put to flight, whole communities wiped out, infrastructure destroyed, records obliterated. Bloss's 'Dinka Madonna' speaks more poignantly than statistics of what has been lost.

Martin Daly

Concordance

Shelf-mark	Catalogue number
Abbott MS 181–202	43
Add. MS 732/60	41
Bamburgh R.2–3	39
Bamburgh Select 6	7
Bamburgh Select 7	17
Bamburgh Select 25	12
Bamburgh Select 83	18
Bamburgh Select 101	22
Cosin A.1.10	29
Cosin D.3.5	33
Cosin MS V.i.1	5
Cosin MS V.i.8	10
Cosin MS V.i.11	6
Cosin MS V.ii.6	3
Cosin MS V.ii.13	13
Cosin MS V.ii.14	15
Cosin MS V.iii.1	4
Cosin MS V.iii.5	14
Cosin MS V.iii.9	11
Cosin MS V.iii.13	8
Cosin MS V.v.6	2
Cosin MS V.v.17	9
Cosin R.1.1	21
Cosin W.5.2	31
Cosin W.5.32	25
Cosin Y.4.6	30
GRE/B46/1/37	40
NSR Planfile C 19/3/1–4	36
OSR Cabinet B1	1
P.Oxy.XII.1582	1
Plomer MS 454	42
Pratt Green X 783.9.FO ENG	48
Routh 3.A.9	16
Routh 14.B.17	27

Shelf-mark	Catalogue number
Routh 14.I2.39	28
Routh 17.D.1	26
Routh 21.B.4	23
Routh 53.C.15	19
Routh 60.A.12	20
Routh 74.C.1	28
SAD 11/9/4	44
SAD 474/10/1	47
SAD 475/3	47
SAD 705/6/7	50
SAD G//S 5/1	46
SAD G//S 628/1	46
SB 0027	32
SB 0300	25
SB 0316	26
SB 0360	28
SB 0366	28
SB 0474	27
SB 2052	49
SB 2396	30
SB+ 0072	24
SB+ 0123	34
SB++ 0018	29
SC 01643	38
SC+ 00043	35
SR.2.B.4	21
SR.2.C.2	20
SR.2.C.11	19
SR.2.D.11	23
SR.3.A.22	24
SR.3.B.1	16
Thomas Wright MS 181/1	37
UMU 144	45

Fragment (both sides shown) from a medieval copy of the so-called Alpha-Beta of Ben Sira, with an interlinear Latin translation, probably dating from the mid-thirteenth century. It was re-used as a hinge-strip in a limp vellum late sixteenth- or early seventeenth-century binding (Portfolio II/4, ex SB 0194: Heinrich Bullinger, Ieremias … CLXX concionibus expositus *(Zurich, 1561)).*

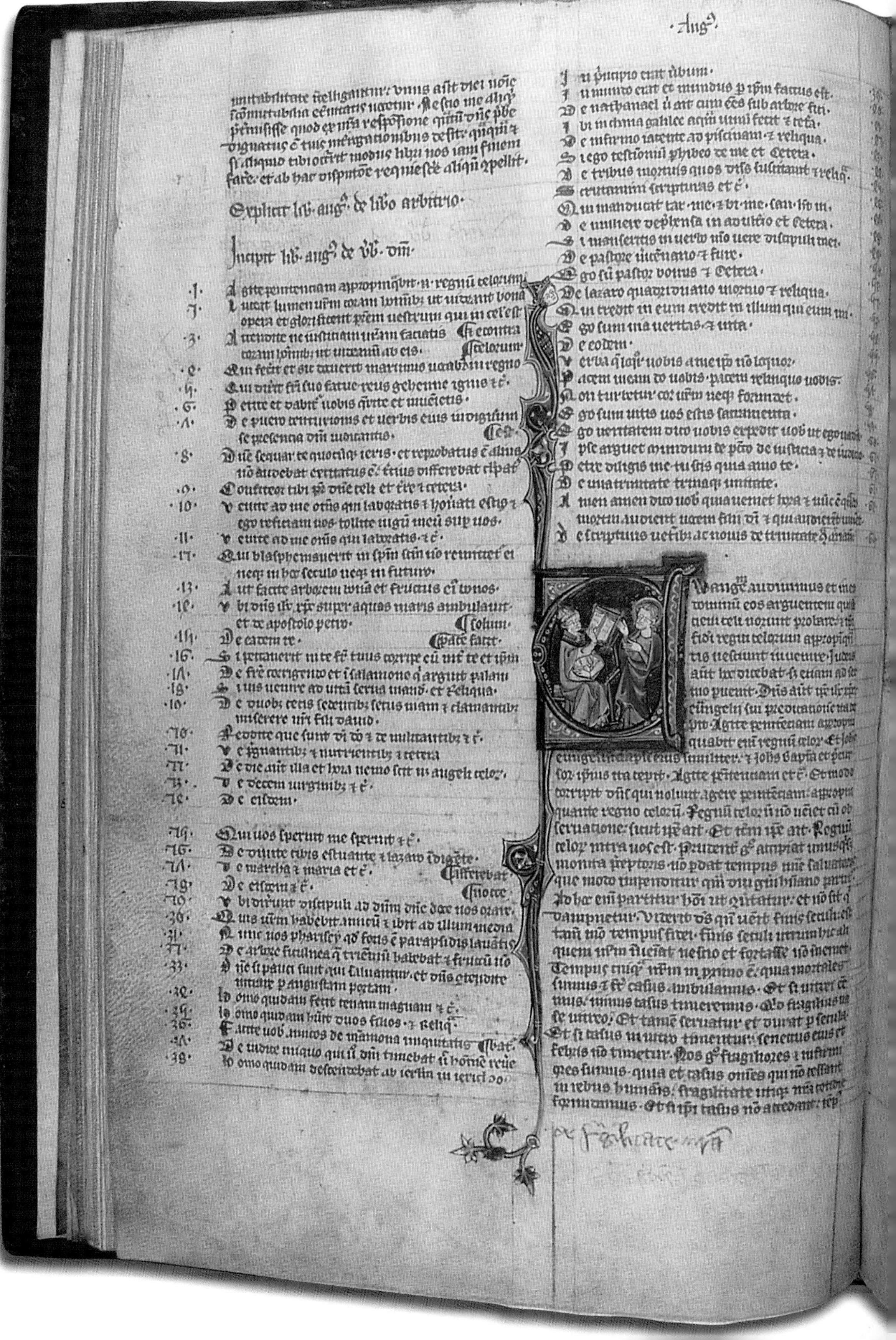

Incipit to Augustine's De uerbis Domini *in the early fourteenth-century, Cosin MS V.i.8* (***no. 10***).

INDEX

Authors, owners, printers, and places of publication of texts and books appear in their place within the alphabetical sequence (but note that medieval individuals are generally indexed under Christian name). The numbers refer to catalogue entries - with the exception of those in italic which refer to pages in the preliminary and ancilliary sections.

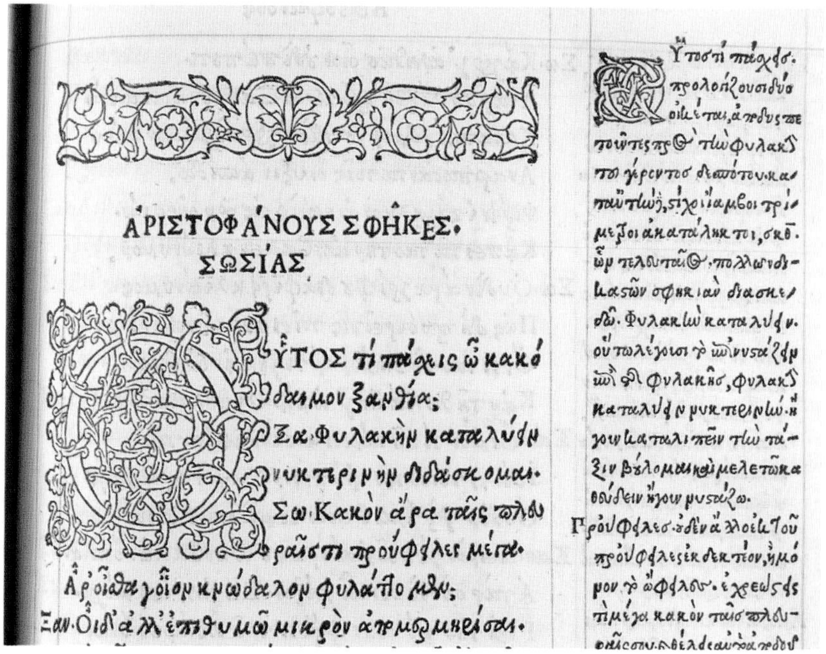
ΑΡΙΣΤΟΦΑΝΟΥΣ ΣΦΗΚΕΣ.
ΣΩΣΙΑΣ.

Beginning of Aristophanes, Wasps *in the Aldine edition of 1498: SR. 2.D.11 (**no. 23**).*

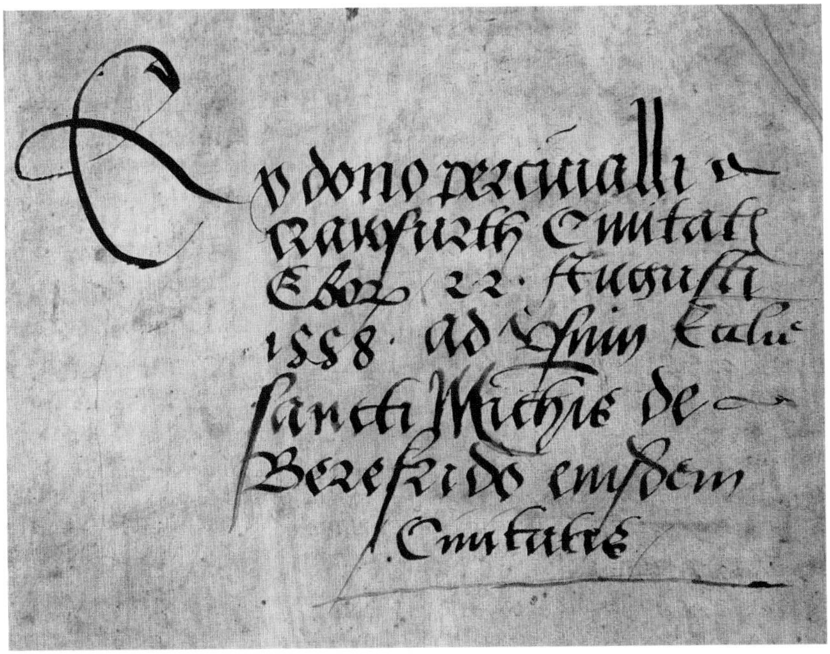

*Inscription added to the 'Holyrood Psalter': 'Given by Percival Crawfurth of the city of York on 22 August 1558 for the use of the church of St Michael le Belfrey of the same city'; Bamburgh Select 6 (**no. 7**).*

Solent qui libros imprimunt autoris laudes vel post libri finem vel ante initiũ collocare. sed cum omnium poetarum latinoꝝ optimus/orator quoqꝫ maximus Publicus Maro Virgilius nõ iniuria ab omnibus predicetur: curam hanc impresentiarum reiicere dignũ duxi. sufficit mihi maiorum testimonium.

Hunc ego Joãnes de Paderborne in westfalia/florentissima in vniuersitate louaniensi residens: ꝙuis non mihi vtilem/in volumine magno ⁊ multa materia diffusum impressi/multorum peritorum instantia victus: qui sic pro quibusdam glosulis inter lineas inserẽdis/saltem his qui nundum in eo initiati erãt opus esse aiebant: non parua data opera vt eum aliis emẽdatiorem ⁊ melius punctis distinctum redderẽ. Finitum itaqꝫ est opus istud per me Joãnem prenotatum meo solito signo consignando/anno ab incarnatione dominica millesimo quadringentesimo septuagesimosexto/mensis aprilis die octaua